FREE MARKET DOGS

THE HUMAN-CANINE BOND IN POST-COMMUNIST POLAND

NEW DIRECTIONS IN THE HUMAN-ANIMAL BOND
Series editors Alan M. Beck and Marguerite E. O'Haire

FREE MARKET DOGS

THE HUMAN-CANINE BOND IN POST-COMMUNIST POLAND

Edited by Michał Piotr Pręgowski and Justyna Włodarczyk

Purdue University Press, West Lafayette, Indiana

Printed in the United States of America.

Library of Congress Cataloging-in-Publication Data

Names: Pręgowski, Michał Piotr, 1978– , editor. | Włodarczyk, Justyna.

Title: Free market dogs : the human-canine bond in post-communist Poland / edited by Michał Piotr Pręgowski and Justyna Włodarczyk.

Description: West Lafayette, Indiana : Purdue University Press, 2016. | Series: New directions in the human-animal bond | Includes bibliographical references and index.

Identifiers: LCCN 2015048694 | ISBN 9781557537409 (pbk. : alk. paper) | ISBN 9781612494517 (epub) | ISBN 9781612494500 (epdf)

Subjects: LCSH: Dogs—Effect of human beings on—Poland.

Classification: LCC SF422.6.P7 F74 2016 | DDC 636.7009438—dc23 LC record available at http://lccn.loc.gov/2015048694

The book is dedicated by Michał to his human family, Kasia, Piotr, and Olaf, and its nonhuman member, Okami—without the latter all this would not have been possible; and by Justyna to the memory of Uma, an extraordinary dog.

Contents

Acknowledgments

This book would not have been possible without the contributions, support, and advice of many people. As editors of this publication, we would like to express our gratitude to those who helped us and provided guidance and encouragement throughout the process of preparing this book. We would particularly like to thank Robert W. Mitchell for his enthusiastic support, genuine interest, and care, as well as his insightful critical feedback for some of the chapters; Alan M. Beck for believing in the value of this publication and supporting our book proposal strongly from the very beginning; and Margo DeMello, Helena Pycior, and Jane Desmond for their encouragement and editorial advice at the preliminary stages of the preparation of this collection. Furthermore, Michał wishes to thank the Council for International Exchange of Scholars, the administrator of the Fulbright Scholar-in-Residence Program, and the Department of Psychology at Eastern Kentucky University, his host in the Scholar-in-Residence program, for the opportunity to work in great comfort on the development of this book.

Additionally, we would like to thank our colleagues from our home universities who have supported us in our animal studies research—Zbigniew Król, Marek Paryż, and Zuzanna Ładyga—as well as Jennifer Drake and Iwona Jakubowska-Branicka, two scholars who have served as long-term sources of inspiration and support. We are also grateful to Tomasz Mońko, Zosia Kwiatkowska, and Dogografia.eu for donating their photographs for this book and to our copy editor, Kelley Kimm, for her enthusiasm and dedication.

Introduction

Michał Piotr Pręgowski and Justyna Włodarczyk

In June 2012 an inconspicuous white Bolognese, a curly lap dog of the Bichon type, became the talk of the town in Poland. Her name was Ramona and someone sent her a small amount of marijuana, drawing attention from the local police. Authorities assumed the drug was in fact meant to reach Olga "Kora" Jackowska, Ramona's guardian and a famed Polish singer. An investigation ensued but was eventually discontinued, predominantly due to the insignificant size of the drug parcel. Nevertheless, Ramona became a *cause célèbre* in the Polish mass media. The case of *Ramona Jackowska,* as the dog was by then officially dubbed, was picked up with excitement by tabloids such as *Fakt* and *Super Express* and gossip websites such as *Pudelek.pl* and *Plotek.pl;* however, even more serious media, such as *NaTemat.pl,* the Polish equivalent of the *Huffington Post,* and *Dziennik* daily, succumbed to the temptation to write about the canine. Surprisingly, it was the latter who, in its entertainment section, reminded Poles about the name day of "the most famous dog of Polish show business" (*Dziennik.pl,* 2012). In journalism ruled by infotainment, sensationalism, and shallow messages, it does not take much to be noticed.

And yet merely 30 years ago Poland and other Eastern European countries were fundamentally different. Not only did dogs of celebrities not make the tabloid headlines in Poland, the Czech Republic, or Bulgaria—there were no tabloids. In fact, there was no freedom of speech either, and censorship gagged the press. The communist era that symbolically ended in Poland in 1989 allowed Poles to reap the benefits of democracy and the capitalist, free market economy. The June 1989 elections and the establishment of the government, led by Solidarity activist Tadeusz Mazowiecki, in September of the same year were the harbingers of tremendous social, cultural, and economic changes in the newly established Third Republic of Poland. For the first time in more than 40 years Poland had a government led by noncommunists, and Polish citizens were once again able to benefit from freedom of speech—as well as from uncontrolled access to American, British, and French press, books, films, art, ideologies, philosophies, and other layers of previously hard-to-reach Western culture.

One of these layers concerns dogs and their role and place in contemporary society, as well as their relationships and interactions with humans. Even though Poles should be considered avid dog lovers—working breeds such as the Polish Greyhound, Polish Hound, Polish Hunting Dog, Polish Lowland Sheepdog, and Polish Tatra Sheepdog were developed in the country centuries ago—the intensity of the socioeconomic changes of the last 25 years strongly influenced how Poles treat their dogs and how emotionally invested they have become in their four-legged companions. Our book is a testament to that change and to the effect the transformation from communism to democracy, and from a state-run economy to a free market economy, has had on Poles and their dogs. Although this collection focuses on Poland alone, numerous remarks and observations can be generalized and may help readers understand the transformation to democracy and its impact on the postcommunist societies of the former Eastern Bloc.

Our decision to prepare a book in English stems from the local success of *Pies też człowiek? Relacje psów i ludzi we współczesnej Polsce* (A dog's life? On humans and canines in contemporary Poland), a book edited by us and published in Poland by Wydawnictwo Naukowe Katedra in March 2014. The volume drew attention from the national, mainstream media, resulting in multiple interviews with authors and editors. The fact that an academic book about human-canine relationships garnered public attention in Poland can be considered a sign of changing times.

The current book comprises heavily expanded versions of articles previously published in Poland, as well as completely new material, absent in the Polish version. In some cases we asked the authors to provide information that would benefit the international audience and to highlight issues that would be particularly interesting to those less familiar with Poland's past and present political, economic, and social situation.

In the first chapter, "Researching the Human-Canine Relationship in Democratic Poland," Michał Piotr Pręgowski and Justyna Włodarczyk provide a detailed look into socioeconomic changes in Poland during and after the transformation, including the post-1989 appearance of premade dog food in Polish stores and the dawn of the popularity of certain North American dog breeds and significant decline in the popularity of other breeds. The authors also present the rise of presidential dogs in Poland (very much in the mold of the "First Dogs" of the United States); the emergence of dog sports (agility, flyball, and rally obedience, among others); issues surrounding dogs in urban spaces, including dog feces (identified as a social issue only in the last decade), as well as the "turf wars" with regard to letting dogs go off leash in municipal parks; and the commercialization of the human-canine relationship in contemporary Poland, as witnessed by the availability of dog-related products and their profound specialization (very much like in the United States and the United Kingdom). The chapter ends with a brief presentation of shelter dogs in Poland and the rising popularity of crossbred dogs, a somewhat new trend adopted *(nomen omen)* by Polish celebrities and ordinary citizens alike.

Agnieszka Orłowska's "Toward Mutual Understanding, Respect, and Trust: On Past and Present Dog Training in Poland" (Chapter 2) is one such enhanced article. Orłowska, an experienced dog trainer certified by the Polish Kennel Club as an assistant for evaluating working trials and conformation shows, looks at both the past and the present, focusing on practical changes in the dog training field in communist and contemporary Poland. As mentioned previously, during communism intellectual and academic exchange with the West was restricted, resulting in local authors becoming key experts (at times, regardless of their actual expertise) and their books the go-to guides for at least two generations of dog keepers. According to Orłowska, the reestablished democracy allowed Poles to access previously unavailable knowledge, and the advent of the Internet in the late 1990s further facilitated a philosophical change from so-called traditional training, a punishment-heavy drill, to positive (nonaversive) training, which is based on rewards and understanding the complicated behavior and cognition of canines. She also introduces the concept of *cynagogy,* urging that dog training is predominantly about education, not control. Orłowska's article is written from the invaluable perspective of a practitioner, someone who has been an active dog trainer for several decades and has had the opportunity to observe firsthand the changes she describes.

Deliberations about dog training are continued in the Chapter 3, "Canine Performance Sports in Poland: Another Look at the Dog Training Revolution," where Justyna Włodarczyk describes how the perception of competitive dog training, and dogs as subjects of such training, have changed since 1989. Włodarczyk discusses the emergence of the myriad previously unavailable canine activities within the context of Poland's transition into a consumer society and analyzes the connection between the positive training revolution and the emergence of the contemporary canine sports scene in Poland. The multidimensional clash of the old with the new concerns topics as fundamental as the role of dogs in these sports, as well as acknowledging (and meeting) their psychological and physical needs in this context. According to Włodarczyk, the contemporary nonaversive approach is more than just an attempt to come up with less intrusive methods of teaching an animal to perform in accordance with the official rules—there is also a genuine desire to fulfill the animal's needs in the competitive sport context. Włodarczyk's article shows how Donna Haraway's understanding of training as "becoming with," an activity that changes both partners and not just the dog (Haraway, 2003), can be applied to the Polish canine sports scene.

Another recent phenomenon is the emergence of the animal-assisted activities (AAA) and animal-assisted therapy (AAT), as presented by Agnieszka Wojtków in Chapter 4, "Dog-Assisted Therapy and Activities in Contemporary Poland." The interest in AAA/AAT developed rather quickly in Poland after the restoration of democracy in 1989. In her chapter, Wojtków presents the local specificity and specialties, at times truly unique, of Polish AAA/AAT organizations. She also covers local pitfalls and controversies, including the irrational overrepresentation of favored breeds in the 1990s and failed efforts to unite the community in the 2000s, as well as the current hot debate surrounding the legal establishment of the professions of *kynoterapeuta* (cynotherapist) and *dogoterapeuta* ("dogotherapist") in 2010. Wojtków, who worked in the dog-assisted therapy field for seven years, urges that the most important goal—that is, the standardization of

AAA and AAT, both their definitions and their understandings, together with establishing a unified set of guidelines—has yet to be reached. The biggest problem is therefore that therapeutic sessions can still be conducted by persons lacking relevant formal education, and often also not knowledgeable enough with regard to canine physiology and behavior.

The issue of knowledge is also present in Małgorzata Rutkowska's "Representations of Dogs in Recent Polish Memoirs and Novels" (Chapter 5). Rutkowska looks at dog memoirs and dog novels as a recent phenomenon in Polish literature, noting that current representations are indebted to Anglo-American cultural products, especially to the sentimental and largely anthropomorphic literary and cinematic depictions of dogs as either charming pets or steadfast companions. Yet for all their similarities, as the author writes, Polish and American dog memoirs and novels differ considerably. In the more famed American dog memoirs—such as Mark Doty's *Dog Years* (Jonathan Cape, 2008) or Jon Katz's *A Good Dog* (Villard Books, 2006)—the dog usually acts as a "savior" to his guardian, changing the course of his or her personal and professional life. In Polish narratives more commonly a man saves a dog and then devotes his time, energy, and money to make the animal healthy and happy again. Moreover, Polish authors focus on the presentation of a dog as part of family life, unlike American authors, who tend to focus on the one-on-one relationship. At the same time, American authors often alternate between reductive anthropomorphism and puzzling otherness in their portrayals of dogs, whereas Polish authors seem to be comfortable mostly with the former perspective: they rarely acknowledge human-animal kinship or ponder the boundary between human and animal worlds, not bothering to question the anthropocentric paradigm.

Dorota Łagodzka takes on the latter topic in Chapter 6, "The Future and the Moment of Animal Suffering in Space: Representations of Laika in Polish Contemporary Art." The author shows how Laika, a Soviet stray dog who became the first animal to orbit the Earth (but not the first animal in space) and, later, the canine icon of bland Eastern Bloc pop culture, is presented in Polish art, which leads to the discussion of more general topics of animal welfare. Łagodzka presents the works of Aleksander Malewski, Agata Zbylut, Kaja Rata, and Zbigniew Rogalski; these works remind us of just how much nonhuman animals have contributed to science, both internationally and locally.

In Chapter 7, "Pet Cemeteries in Poland and Beyond: Their Histories, Meanings, and Symbolism," Michał Piotr Pręgowski discusses a relatively new social practice in Poland: burying deceased companion animals in pet cemeteries. The first Polish pet cemetery was established in 1991, two years after the fall of the Iron Curtain and almost 100 years after the establishment of the Hartsdale Pet Cemetery in the suburbs of New York. This is not to say that pet cemeteries are now common in Poland; as Pręgowski writes, in 2015 the nation of 38.5 million people had 12 official pet cemeteries at their disposal, merely 1 per 3.2 million citizens, whereas in the United States there is roughly 1 per 0.5 million citizens. At the same time the phenomenon is clearly on the rise, as witnessed by the recent opening of a pet cemetery near Rzeszów (co-funded by the European Union), as well as by the ongoing talks with local authorities in at least five other big cities, including Cracow. Pręgowski discusses similarities and differences between Polish and American pet cemeteries, as well as between pet cemeteries and human cemeteries in general. As Stanley Brandes aptly notes, burying beloved animals in specifically designated public places demonstrates extraordinary devotion and attributes a degree of sacredness to them (Brandes, 2009). Even though pet cemeteries are a resting place of only a fraction of Polish companion animals so far, the rising awareness of their existence cannot go unnoticed. The graves and gravestones of deceased canines allow a glimpse into the intimate world humans share with them: Pręgowski describes social practices connected with pet cemeteries, and discusses the use of religious symbols and other means of expressing belief in an afterlife for animals, as well as ways of commemorating dogs (routinely presented as best friends in Poland and as members of the family in the United States). He also indicates that Poles, just like Americans and members of other Western nations, adhere to congruent social rituals after losing four-legged friends. As such, the rise of the pet cemetery in Poland is an ultimate testament to the impact the transition to democracy has had on the human-canine bond in the Third Republic.

References

Brandes, S. (2009). The meaning of American pet cemetery gravestones, *Ethnology, 48*(2), 99–118.

Dziennik.pl. (2012, August 31). Najsłynniejszy pies polskiego show biznesu świętuje imieniny [The most famous dog in polish show business celebrates its name day]. Retrieved from http://rozrywka.dziennik.pl/plotki/galeria/402751,1,najslynniejszy-pies-polskiego-show-biznesu-swietuje-imieniny-galeria-zdjec-galeria-zdjec.html [Accessed 23 May 2015].

Haraway, D. (2003). *Companion species manifesto: Dogs, people and significant otherness.* Chicago, IL: Prickly Paradigm Press.

Pręgowski, M. P., & Włodarczyk, J. (2014). *Pies też człowiek? Relacje ludzi i psów we współczesnej Polsce* [A dog's life? On humans and dogs in contemporary Poland]. Gdańsk, Poland: WN Katedra.

Four Paws of the Third Republic of Poland: A Timeline

1989

- The Round Table talks between the ruling Polish United Workers' Party and the democratic opposition start on February 6 in Warsaw.
- The Round Table Agreement is signed on April 4. Its key resolutions include (1) legalization of independent trade unions, (2) introduction of the office of President elected in citizen voting (thereby annulling the power of the Communist Party General Secretary), and (3) establishment of the Senate, the upper house of the Polish parliament.
- People's Republic of Poland, the official name of the communist state, becomes the Republic of Poland, also known as the Third Republic of Poland, on December 31.

1990

- *Reksio,* a famous TV animated series about a little dog of the same name, one of the all-time favorites in Poland, is discontinued after 33 years of production.
- Lech Wałęsa, the cofounder of the self-governing trade union, *Solidarność* (Solidarity), and the Nobel Peace Prize winner in 1983, becomes the president of Poland on December 22.

1991

- The first Polish pet cemetery, *Psi los* (A Dog's Life), opens its premises in Konik Nowy near Warsaw.
- The first issue of *Mój Pies* (My dog) monthly magazine hits the stands.

1992

- Pedigree Pal, the American dry and wet dog food owned by Mars, Inc., debuts on the Polish market.

1993

- World Animal Day, an international day of action for animal rights and welfare, is celebrated in Poland for the first time.

1994

- John Fisher's *Think Dog!* (Okiem psa) becomes the first non-Polish dog training bestseller in the country.

1995

- Ewa Szulc publishes one of the first Polish dog memoirs, *I kto tu szczeka?* (Who is barking?).

1996

- Maria Czerwińska, the founder and the president of *Fundacja Przyjaźni Ludzi i Zwierząt "Cze-ne-ka"* (Foundation for Human and Animal Friendship "Cze-ne-ka"), coins the term *dogoterapia* (dog-assisted therapy: literally, "dog therapy") to describe activities taking place between her dogs and patients.
- The Nobel Prize in Literature is awarded to poet Wisława Szymborska, a cat lover.

1997

- The Constitution of the Third Republic of Poland is adopted by the National Assembly on April 2.

1999

- Poland officially joins the North Atlantic Treaty Organization (NATO) on March 12.
- Kakadu, the biggest Polish pet supply chain similar to PetSmart, opens its first store in Janki near Warsaw.

- Barbara Waldoch, a Polish-Australian dog trainer, establishes an online discussion group, *Kliker*, to promote reward-based training methods in Poland.

2000

- Film director Andrzej Wajda is presented with an honorary Oscar for his contribution to world cinema at the Academy Awards gala.

2001

- The first seminar with well-known Norwegian positive reinforcement trainer Turid Rugaas is organized in Warsaw. The seminar paves the way for inviting more Western dog training experts to come to Poland to teach about positive training.

2003

- Poland and nine other countries sign the Treaty of Accession with the member states of the European Union.

2004

- Poland officially accesses the European Union and becomes a member country.
- The *Polski Związek Dogoterapii* (Polish Dogotherapy Association) is created to establish countrywide standards inspired by the Delta Society.
- The first obedience competition is organized in Błażejewko near Poznań according to a set of newly adopted international rules.
- *Polityka* weekly publishes a long article about Violetta Villas, an internationally recognized singer and diva, who became an animal hoarder after retirement. Villas is portrayed as a troubled woman with a heart of gold.

2005

- *Ludzie i ich zwierzęta. Interakcjonistyczno—symboliczna analiza społecznego świata właścicieli zwierząt domowych* (People and their animals: An interactionist-symbolic analysis of the social world of companion animal owners), a sociological take on our relationships with companion animals,

predominantly dogs, is published by Krzysztof Tomasz Konecki.
- PZU S.A., the biggest insurance company in Poland, introduces a companion-animal-oriented product, *Cztery Łapy* (Four Paws).

2006

- Cartoonist Marek Raczkowski performs an artistic provocation by placing miniature Polish flags into dog feces in Warsaw's city parks. His action, aimed at raising awareness of the "poop problem," is offensive to some and subsequently investigated by the public prosecutor in a possible case of profaning national symbols.

2007

- *Mój Pies* monthly, together with its readers, initiates the annual event *Zerwijmy łańcuchy* (Let's Break the Chains), aimed at educating society about the welfare of dogs in rural Poland.

2009

- Jerzy Buzek, former prime minister of Poland (1997–2001), becomes president of the European Parliament, one of the highest officials in the European Union.
- The *Polskie Stowarzyszenie Groomerów* (Polish Association of Groomers) begins its operation; sets popularizing grooming as a profession as one of its key goals.

2010

- After the tragic death of president Lech Kaczyński and his wife Maria in a plane crash near Smoleńsk on April 10, Polish tabloids investigate the future awaiting the presidential couple's dogs and gladly spread the news that they found new homes.
- The professions of *kynoterapeuta* (cynotherapist) and *dogoterapeuta* ("dogotherapist") are officially established. Animal-assisted therapy practitioners and sympathizers are divided; some members of the community are wary of potential animal welfare problems connected to making dog-assisted therapy a main source of income and a full-time job, while others criticize the lack of countrywide standards.

2011

- Rally obedience (Rally-O), a "lifestyle sport" born in the United States and a fun-oriented version of well-known competitive obedience, makes its debut on the Polish canine sports scene.
- The *Związek Kynologiczny w Polsce* (Polish Kennel Club) bans the registration as well as showing of dogs with cropped ears and docked tails.

2012

- Olga Kwiecień and her Pyrenean Shepherd, Brava, are the first Polish competitors to win a medal at the Fédération Cynologique Internationale (FCI) Agility World Championships in Liberec, Czech Republic.
- Poland hosts the European Championships in canine disc dog sport, gathering over 300 participants from around the world.
- Ramona, a lap dog of a famed singer, Kora, becomes a hot topic for the tabloids after someone addresses a small package of marijuana to her. Ramona is soon dubbed "the most famous dog of Polish show business."

2013

- *Psi los* in Konik Nowy becomes the resting place of a 10,000th companion animal.
- Euromonitor International reports that in 2012 Poles spent more than 1.8 billion Polish Zloty—the equivalent of roughly 480 million USD—on pet food alone.

2014

- Donald Tusk, former prime minister of Poland (2007–2014), becomes president of the European Council, a principal representative of the European Union on the world stage, on December 1.
- The top Polish flyball team, Unleashed Blade Runners, wins the European Flyball Championships in France.

2015

- The mayor of Warsaw announces the start of a fully refunded spay and neuter program for companion animals; Warsaw dwellers get the opportunity to spay and neuter their dogs for free.

1

Researching the Human-Canine Relationship in Democratic Poland

Michał Piotr Pręgowski and Justyna Włodarczyk

Is it legitimate to claim that Poland's systemic transformation of 1989, the shift from communism to democracy, was also a turning point in Poles' relationships with dogs? While the date itself has a mostly symbolic significance, the conditions created by the reestablished democracy and free market capitalism have had a very direct effect on the lives of dogs, to a large extent because their guardians are also potential voters and consumers, and because the fact that Poles share their lives with dogs is increasingly becoming a significant element of their identity as citizens of a democratic state.

Most of the recent research that tries to take stock of the changes in human-animal relationships after World War II comes from—and pertains to—countries that were located to the west of the Iron Curtain. In fact, the adjectives *contemporary* and *modern* (not to mention *postmodern*) function, in common parlance, as stand-ins for "Western liberal democracy" and by default exclude the totalitarian regimes that covered almost half of the territory of Europe until the early 1990s. It seems that both democracy and capitalism have been taken for granted as a certain starting point for the analysis of the human-animal bond. While the effects of capitalism on the lives of animals have been discussed by Western scholars in a mostly negative light—with the oppressive practices of factory farming, tied to capitalism's drive for greater productiveness and efficiency, leading to the commodification of farm animals (Novek, 2005; Shukin, 2009) and the concurrent fetishization of family pets in a consumer society (Herzog, 2010)—this chapter, and the book in general, offers a somewhat different perspective. While not glorifying capitalism, it traces the changes in the status of dogs alongside the rapid development of a capitalist economy, bringing certain connections to the surface and leaving it up to the reader to evaluate whether dogs (and which dogs) are better off in a capitalist system.

Similarly, this book also brings to the forefront the role played by democracy and, as a corollary, the civic engagement that is a trademark of democratic societies. While pet-keeping is by no means restricted to democratic states, it comes as no surprise that both its symbolic functions and the everyday practices associated with it are quite different in a totalitarian regime than in a democratic society. Furthermore, the very notion of animal rights, a notion which is entangled with the recent changes in the human-animal bond, though not in a univocal way, seems relevant only in a society which values the notion of human rights. It will become clear that in the case of Poland—and Poland here can serve as a representative example for the former Eastern Bloc—activism related to animals is influenced by Poles' increased feelings of agency as citizens of a democratic republic. In the canine case such activism consists of lobbying to change laws related to animal welfare (including leash and muzzle laws), as well as grassroots initiatives connected to the establishment of dog parks. In fact, animal-related and environmental activism has become one of the fields which make it possible to trace the disappearance of the passive *Homo sovieticus,* who grudgingly accepts reality "as is," doubting that it can be influenced in any way.

This book reveals Poles' increasing emotional involvement with their dogs and, even more importantly, their growing desire to understand these nonhuman animals and the bond which binds them together. By no means do we claim that Poles did not love their dogs before 1989, or that they did not share their homes with them. Yet, somehow, a book like this one, one that goes beyond being either a "care and training handbook" for dog guardians or a photograph album, would have been inconceivable in Poland 25 years ago. Most Poles simply kept dogs as pets and the vocabularies they used to describe them were those of biology and veterinary medicine. Here, we consciously apply the methodologies of different disciplines from the humanities—sociology, anthropology, literary studies, history, gender studies, cultural studies, and pedagogy—to answer questions about the character of the human-canine bond.

The birth of this book owes a lot to what has been described as "the animal turn" (Ritvo, 2007; Weil, 2010) within the humanities and social sciences and the establishment of the fields of animal studies, human-animal studies, and anthrozoology. This interest in animals, the human-animal bond, and the questioning of the human/animal boundary that comes with it has recently begun to impact Polish academia, and the past few years have witnessed the publication of the first books written from an animal studies perspective (Krzysztof Konecki's *Ludzie i ich zwierzęta* [People and their animals], 2005; Monika Bakke's *Bio-transfiguracje* [Bio-transfigurations], 2012; and several anthologies[1]) and the organization of international conferences, as well as visits and lectures by prolific animal studies scholars, including Peter Singer in 2012. However, these events and publications date back no more than a decade, and it is only in the last few years (post-2010) where we can locate a true rise of interest. The fact that the animal turn was delayed in reaching Eastern Europe suggests that certain preconditions need to be in place before interest in animal studies can develop. While we may claim that these preconditions are primarily intellectual—that is, that scholars need to become acquainted with certain theories and methodologies—there is no question that there are clear economic and political dimensions involved.

The following anecdote will serve as an illustration. The first issue of the current most popular daily newspaper in Poland, *Gazeta Wyborcza*, was published in May 1989, before the first free elections, and was one of the first widely available censorship-free publications in Poland. In May of 2014 the editors of *Gazeta Wyborcza* took their readers down memory lane and reissued some of the news items published exactly 25 years previously in other daily publications. The leading story in the newspaper *Dziennik Polski* on 8 May 1989, had concerned the world's largest dog, a purebred (breed not mentioned) animal from London, weighing in at 149 kilograms. The story claimed the dog consumed 5 kilograms of meat per day. The headline of the article read, "Two Food Ration Stamps a Day!" (Lipiński, 2014). In the Poland of the 1980s, meat and other grocery products were rationed: each citizen received a specific number of stamps which they could use to buy desired products. Meat was a strictly rationed luxury with 1 kilogram (approximately 2 pounds) of meat per month assigned—though not necessarily available—to each citizen. The very possibility of a dog consuming the equivalent of a human's five-month ration of meat in one day was deemed an inconceivable extravagance. On the other hand, a society in which a scenario such as this could truly come to life loomed as the fulfillment of dreams: as paradise. The struggle for everyday survival in a communist economy created different material conditions relating to household pets than those in affluent Western societies.

This is not to say that there was no interest in companion animals in pre-1989 Poland, but that the preconditions for the modern preoccupation with animals were not there. However, the current explosion of interest in animals in the former Eastern Bloc suggests that the dominant explanations for the animal turn may have to be redefined to include accounts that do not follow the Western (often Anglo-Saxon) narrative. After the interlude of totalitarian rule, modernity and postmodernity—carrying very different attitudes toward animals with them—hit the Eastern bloc almost simultaneously. For example, in *Animals and Modern Cultures* Adrian Franklin discusses the shift in human relations to animals as connected not just to the shift from modernity to postmodernity, but from a Fordist economy to a post-Fordist economy (Franklin, 1999). It is this specific economic change that Franklin sees as responsible for creating aspects of the postmodern condition that he enumerates as key for the shift in the status of animals: misanthropy, risk, and ontological insecurity (Franklin, 1999, p. 3). One may ask what if the shift was not from Fordism to post-Fordism but from communism to a very "Wild East" version of capitalism. In other words, what if the results are similar but the processes that led to them were different? This is one of the questions tackled by this book.

A Friend or a Nuisance?

Why focus solely on dogs, though? The reasons are twofold. First, as the editors of this collection we are particularly interested in dogs as companions: we share our lives with them and they happen to be the animals we have the most experience with. However, focusing on dogs is not just a personal preference; rather, our personal preference is representative of Poles' general preference. Although Poland lacks all-encompassing, methodologically sound, nationwide data, from the bits of information gathered from institutions such as the Supreme Audit Office (*Najwyższa Izba Kontroli*, the entity that most Polish animal shelters respond to) and the Polish Society for the Care of Animals (*Towarzystwo Opieki nad Zwierzętami w Polsce*, which estimates the number of animals in Polish households) one can assume that dogs are the most popular companion animal in Poland. More importantly, dogs accompany people in public spaces and subsequently are subject to legal and customary "turf wars"; dog feces is litter, but the excrement of indoor-outdoor cats is not. Changes in Poles' relationships to dogs are also representative of broader processes that can be explored using the microcosm of *dogland* (to use a term introduced by Donna Haraway [2008] and less emotionally loaded than the often condescendingly applied *dog fancy*). In light of the complexity of the various activities humans engage in with dogs, the dog is also the animal with which Poles enter into the deepest and most multidimensional relations. Not only do Poles refer to the dog as "man's best friend"—a saying as popular in the Polish language as it is in English—but they also declare, as Krzysztof Konecki's research reveals, that they believe dogs are predisposed to bonding with humans (97.2 percent of respondents agreed, compared with 44.1 percent in response to the same statement about cats; Konecki, 2005, p. 210). Many Poles treat dogs as family members, although they do not necessarily refer to them as such; regardless of the latter, dogs accompany Poles during various family celebrations and events, and families often modify their preferences for engaging in social activities in a way that acknowledges the family dog.

Human-canine interactions do not, however, always take place in a friendly atmosphere and in safe surroundings. The dog, as a domestic animal encountered increasingly in urban and suburban space, brings to the forefront the arbitrariness of nature/culture and wild/tame distinctions. At the same time, attitudes toward dogs can reflect the fears connected with the blurring of these boundaries. This is why in recent years canines have also become a source of conflict among Poland's urban dwellers. Those who see dogs as important life companions want to share their life and living space with them; others consider the presence of dogs in shared public space a nuisance or even something unbearable. Although dogs are increasingly present in urban spaces (dog-friendly restaurants and shops are being established in many large cities), there is also a strong negative reaction to this presence, an anti-dog backlash. According to estimates (and yet again, estimates only) of the Polish Association for Animal Identification and Registration, there are 9 dogs for every 100 humans in Polish cities (Piątek, 2015, p. 32). No wonder peaceful coexistence has become such a hot topic.

A discussion that took place in the summer of 2013 in the local Warsaw supplement to *Gazeta Wyborcza* and in the related online forum is an excellent example of the gist—and the language—of this conflict. The debate began when a letter was published from a canine guardian complaining about discrimination after one of her favorite parks had banned dogs from its grounds. As the author demanded what she viewed as justice for her dog, she made an appeal in the language of human rights, extending the scope of human rights discourse to another species. Specifically, she referred to "discrimination," "exclusion," and "right to spontaneity" (*Gazeta Wyborcza Stołeczna,* 2013). Readers responded to the letter with an explosion of either support or hostility, clothed in emotionally loaded language. The opponents of dogs' presence in urban areas had rightly pointed out that Polish cities were not designed with dogs in mind and that barking can be a nuisance; some also tried to impute that dogs constitute a grave health risk for the city-dwelling population.

Yet it is not just the arguments that are striking here but the way in which they were presented. One of the readers summed it all up in six words: "Filth, foul stench, parasites and bacteria!,"[2] while another reader, who lived one floor below a dog-owning household, added that "apartments are not made for containing these 100-pound beasts that need to roam."

Dogs are an increasing presence in the urban cityscape. (Copyright by K9Action [Tomasz Mońko], www.k9action.eu. Courtesy of Tomasz Mońko.)

The problem with this particular "beast"—a Golden Retriever—was that the dog's claws made a sound as they came into contact with the hardwood floors. Discussions like this one inevitably lead back to the argument of personal privacy and bodily autonomy: "If you want to have a dog, sure thing, as long as it wears a diaper and doesn't come in contact with anyone who does not wish to have the air polluted by your dog." The final straw is usually the pseudo-humanitarian argument: "And who would want to keep a dog in the city anyway? Dogs suffer in the city."

The sharp tone of these value judgments, most likely additionally strengthened in light of the anonymity offered by the Internet, recalls the language of what has come to be known in the United States as the "culture war"—that is, a conflict over the fundamental values structuring society (Hunter, 1992).

A possible hypothesis regarding why this conflict has reached such a scale in post-1989 Poland pertains to the country's chronology of human-animal relations. As previously stated, modernity and postmodernity impacted post-communist Poland at the same time, which seems to have exacerbated certain conflicts that never had the chance to escalate in other parts of the world. As many scholars have argued, modernity is characterized by greater separation of humans and animals (Atkins, 2012; Baker, 2000; Franklin, 1999; see also Bulliet's [2005] notions of domesticity and post-domesticity). Steve Baker writes that "the animal is the first thing to be ruled out of modernism's bounds" (Baker, 2000, p. 20). It is also generally agreed upon that the modernist (and modern) impulse is to classify, design taxonomies, and then organize space in a way that reflects these taxonomies. In *Animal Cities* Peter Atkins shows how animals' association with filth and disease contributed to their relegation outside of city limits. Modernization became synonymous with getting rid of animals from the cityscape, justified through fears related to hygiene and public safety. The gradual shift to postmodernism's valuation of emotional attachment to animals provided time for urban communities to establish rules according to which some animals could be readmitted into shared public space. The period after 1989 in Poland is marked simultaneously by modernity's desire to cleanse and postmodernism's desire for close emotional attachments with animals. Communist Poland missed out on some of these modernizing strategies: most importantly, it never even attempted to tackle the issue of dog waste.

The solution to these mounting tensions will not be quick and simple and will require further cultural changes. It is difficult to not notice that the still unresolved issue of canine feces on city streets and sidewalks is not helping the cause of canine enthusiasts. It is hard to deny that Poles have not yet caught up with the West when it comes to cleaning up after their dogs. This Polish specificity has been mocked by, for example, political cartoonist and artist Marek Raczkowski, who, during a March 24, 2006, interview for Radio TOK FM, admitted to the artistic provocation of inserting miniature Polish flags into dog feces found in city parks in Warsaw. When a recording of this artistic happening was broadcast by the TVN television channel on March 25, 2008, the public prosecutor became interested and investigated it as a possible case of profaning a national symbol.

Meanwhile, the association of cleaning up after a dog with modernity is deliberately used as a strategy in campaigns advocating the practice. City authorities and dog guardians have cooperated in organizing campaigns promoting the cleanup of dog feces; strategies have included publicizing via large billboards and small leaflets, distributing pet waste bags, and increasing the number of trash cans in city parks. Interestingly, in addition to reinforcing the notion of personal responsibility (one of the largest nationwide campaigns is bluntly titled "Your Dog—Your Poop"), the promotional materials associate cleaning up after a dog with caring for public space and even present it as an allegory of modern patriotism. For example, a popular children's book *A ja jestem Polak mały* (I am a little Pole) defines patriotism as consideration for others and includes cleaning up after a dog in its list of positive examples, along with recycling and segregating garbage (Piotrowska, 2014).

Media Animals

In post-communist countries the dog has become something of a go-to nonhuman species for the mass media. While an analysis of the media representations of dogs does not bring us any closer to understanding the canine mind, it can tell us a lot about a society's prevalent social values. Despite Poles' declared emotional attachment to their companion animals, dogs are rarely presented in the media with emphasis on their unique character. They are mostly noted for being the embodiment of representativeness—for example, canine loyalty or courage—or for their association with famous people. Until about the 1950s, however, the most recognizable Polish companion animal was the chestnut mare owned in the interwar period by Józef Piłsudski (1867–1935), Polish chief of state and the First Marshal of Poland. The mare, Kasztanka, was immortalized in countless songs and photographs. It was during the period of the communist Polish People's Republic (1952–1989) that canines became more visible in the media, but they were mostly fictitious characters, such as the German

Shepherds Szarik and Cywil from popular TV series, as well as terrier-like Reksio from the TV animated series by the same title and a somewhat nondescript, spaniel-like puppet named Pankracy from a children's program of the 1970s and 1980s.

Szarik, the canine character from the television series *Czterej pancerni i pies* (Four tank-men and a dog), is a particularly interesting case here. The wildly popular series, which ran from 1966 to 1970 and was based on a young adult novel, was entangled in the political project of the Polish People's Republic; that is, its goal was to make clear that the Red Army had been an ally of Poland throughout World War II, overlooking the reality of the Ribbentrop–Molotov Pact. The episodes followed the adventures of four soldiers and comrades of different nationalities fighting together against the Nazis. The soldiers were accompanied by Szarik, an incredibly smart dog whose unbelievable feats of courage and loyalty constituted a significant theme in the series. Szarik was clearly based on the famous Rin Tin Tin and should assume an honorary place in the tradition of military German Shepherds in film. As explored by Aaron Skabelund (2014), combat dogs in war movies are almost without exception German Shepherds, a breed that has come to connote courage, sagacity, and the kind of hypermasculinity associated with war combat. Thus, even though in the book Szarik is described as a Laika (the writer's decision to use a Russian breed was most likely another propagandist element), a German Shepherd stars in the TV version. As Skabelund argues elsewhere, despite their strong association with the Nazis in the second half of the 20th century, German Shepherds were a pliable symbol of colonial rule as protectors, deterrents, and enforcers of social control (Skabelund, 2008), and here Szarik played in the interests of Soviet colonial rule. To bypass the association with the Nazis, particularly problematic in postwar Poland, Szarik was referred to in the film series as an "Alsatian Shepherd" because the French region of Alsace-Lorraine had been occupied by the Nazis and forcibly incorporated into the Third Reich.

Szarik became something of a cult figure and was at least partly responsible for the huge popularity of German Shepherds in the People's Republic of Poland. Szarik was played by a dog named Trymer (and some doubles), who, upon death, was stuffed, mounted, and placed on display at the police dog training school in Sułkowice, where he had been trained. The popularity of the TV series also, though rather briefly, put dog training into the spotlight as interviews with Szarik's trainer, Franciszek Szydełko, were published (and still are!) in the media. Szydełko went on to train animals for most movies created in the People's Republic of Poland, including the famed *Przygody psa Cywila* (The adventures of Cywil), another Rin Tin Tin–like series about an unusually smart police dog.

While TV series about military/police German Shepherds live on—yet another season of *Komisarz Alex* (Commissioner Alex), a spinoff of *Rex, a Cop's Best Friend,* was still being filmed in Poland in 2015—the popularity of modern-day canine television characters is nowhere near that of Szarik. In fact, the most famous canines in contemporary Poland are those who become well known through their association with people, mostly celebrities and politicians.

In this, social reality after 1989 brings Poland closer to English-speaking Western countries, which are a potent source of inspiration for contemporary Poland. In the United States, dogs have been White House residents continuously for more than 100 years—that is, since the presidency of Theodore Roosevelt (1901–1909)—while the first presidential canine to achieve national fame was the Scottish Terrier Fala, a pet of president Franklin Delano Roosevelt. Roosevelt and Fala were almost inseparable and their bond became legendary. Mark Derr, the author of *A Dog's History of the United States,* notes that the president consciously turned to a smaller dog because he wanted to be able to take his dog on presidential trips. Derr also emphasizes that the vigor and energy exuded by Fala assured the nation that the disabled president was a capable man: If the dog was happy, it was clear that the president could cope with his duties (Derr, 2004, pp. 305–306). Fala unwittingly inaugurated what has become something of an institution: the function of "America's First Dog." Some presidents, such as Bill Clinton and Barack Obama, only acquired dogs after they moved into the White House, which, as Derr notes, suggests that their decision may have been less a result of a personal affinity for dogs and more of a publicity move. Nevertheless, it remains a fact that the families of U.S. leaders, regardless of their political orientation, now remain incomplete without a dog.

In the United Kingdom, the tradition of royal dogs has even deeper roots. Queen Victoria was known for setting up kennels at Windsor and breeding different breeds of dogs (Rappaport 2003, pp. 34–39), while Queen Elizabeth is known for her love of short-legged corgis. The difference between the attitude of the British monarchs and American presidents seems a reflection of the differences in the two countries' political systems: in the United Kingdom the monarchs are engaged in breeding valuable dogs, that is, in taking care of a canine "dynasty," while in the United States the democratically elected presidents are not outwardly involved in creating their own "lines."[3] In fact, it is public knowledge that President Obama's Bo and Sunny are spayed and neutered.

Polish presidents seem to be taking their cue from their American counterparts. The first dogs in the Polish Presidential Palace were the German Shepherds owned by Aleksander Kwaśniewski, the second (after Lech Wałęsa) popularly elected president of the Third Republic of Poland. However, it was only during the presidency of Lech Kaczyński that the popular media became interested in the four-legged inhabitants of the Polish equivalent of the White House. When the presidential couple's dog Tytus died in 2009, the media sympathetically portrayed their grief, although a few months later, in early 2010, local tabloids asked their readers if they wanted the Presidential Palace to be "defended" by Lula or "taken over" by Draka, the spaniel of Bronisław and Anna Komorowski (cf. *Super Express,* 2010). After the tragic death of Lech and Maria Kaczyński in an airplane crash near Smoleńsk later that year (on April 10, 2010), the same tabloids speculated, quite seriously, about what would happen to the couple's dogs and then informed with satisfaction about how the animals were doing in their new homes (cf. *Fakt,* 2010).

The presidency of Bronisław Komorowski (2010–2015), an enthusiast of hunting dogs (and formerly of hunting as well, a hobby he publicly gave up after being elected), made it possible for the media's fascination with presidential pets to continue. Komorowski's spaniel Draka, nicknamed Punia, has become the hero of multiple articles published in the popular press. The press has informed about the presidential couple providing a good example for fellow countrymen by cleaning up after their dog; tabloids are also keen to provide anecdotes about unusual events involving the presidential dog (more recently, dogs; interestingly, since Komorowski became president in 2010, the family has grown larger and now includes three canines). In 2010 Draka spontaneously greeted Queen Sylvia in front of the Belvedere Palace during the Swedish royal couple's visit to Poland (cf. *Super Express*, 2011). As reported in *Fakt* (2011a), the president's canine "greets royal guests, takes part in important meetings and attends almost all conferences. If you visit the head of state ... you need to meet Draka and make sure she likes you."

These descriptions vividly recall the media interest expressed by the British and American tabloids in their First Dogs. Possibly, the Polish media will soon openly expect each subsequent president to keep a four-legged companion in the Presidential Palace.

What changes in the Polish public sphere have made the issue of pet-keeping relevant for a politician? Why is it that caring for an animal—rather than *having* an animal—is perceived as praiseworthy and socially significant? Certainly the answers to these questions are related to the reestablishment, or establishment, of democracy, a system wherein politicians must worry about being elected and reelected to office and creating and maintaining a positive media image. Understandably this concern was absent in communist Poland and other countries of the Eastern Bloc. Yet public relations is only a partial answer, for it still does not tackle the question as to why a pet dog can make a difference in a politician's persona. Media emphasis tends to center on dogs because no other companion animal completes a politician's image quite the way a dog does. The effect of a pet dog is the softening of a politician's image in a way that reveals his—or her, but usually his—more empathetic and gentler side. After all, it is easier to see a caring human being in someone who likes animals, even if we do not share this person's political views. The fact that these values are significant in post-communist Poland shows that the notion of "the sentimental citizen"—a citizen who makes political decisions on the basis of emotional preferences—discussed in the American context by George E. Marcus (2002) in *The Sentimental Citizen: Emotion in Democratic Politics*, is not solely American after all. It therefore should come as no surprise that in 2012 the photograph that gathered the most "likes" on the Polish Prime Minister's official Facebook page was a photograph of Prime Minister Donald Tusk hugging his dog Szeryf.

One of the recurring motifs in this book is a microscale analysis of Poles' adaptation of the cultural models typical for Anglo-Saxon countries on the level of their relations to dogs. While this trend may have been based on a certain preexisting fascination, it was enabled by specific political and economic changes after 1989: the reintroduction of democracy and of the free market economy, including Poland's almost instant immersion in the processes of globalization. Young capitalism, in connection with the development of information technologies and Poles' growing access to the Internet in the first decade of the 21st century, had a huge effect on Poles' relationships with their dogs.

The Free Market Dog

It is difficult to ascertain whether the newly established capitalism of former Eastern Bloc countries shapes or reflects people's relationships to their dogs, but it remains a fact that in a free market economy dogs are becoming increasingly more important as consumers (even if their decision-making capacities are somewhat restricted because it is their guardians who are paying). The past two decades were a period of dynamic expansion in the pet accessories market in Poland and neighboring countries, particularly in the area of pet foods. The practice of feeding dogs table scraps is long gone—particularly in urban areas and among those who consider themselves urban dwellers. The news tidbit from 1989—about a super-sized dog consuming 5 kilograms of meat per day—would not make headlines today because the availability of meat is commonplace. However, before 1989 Polish translations of Western books about dogs would routinely skip the chapters on dog foods or adapt them to the condition of the Eastern Bloc. For example, Jan Grabowski, in his time a well-known breeder of hunting dogs and the translator of German author's Manfred Koch-Kostersitz's book *400 Ratschläge für den Hundefreund* (400 tips for dog lovers), added a long footnote to the diet section of the Polish edition. Where Koch-Kostersitz focused on commercially produced pet foods unavailable in communist

Poland, Grabowski proposed a diet of bread rolls soaked in milk with an addition of vegetable oil (Koch-Kostersitz, 1988, p. 30).

Today dog guardians in Poland can choose from several dozen brands of specialized dog foods, ranging from mass-market Pedigree Pal and other brands from global moguls such as Procter & Gamble, Nestlé, and Mars, to super premium holistic and hypoallergenic products offered by small entities such as the UK-based family-run Natural Dog Food Company. Euromonitor International, a private London-based research company providing market analyses and business intelligence reports, recently reported that in 2012 Poles spent more than 1.8 billion Polish Zloty—the equivalent of roughly 480 million USD—on pet food alone (*Gazeta Wyborcza,* 2014). Euromonitor International also estimated that by 2015 Polish homes would host 6.1 million cats and more than 7.8 million dogs and that Poles are spending gradually more money on all-encompassing companion animal care.

Marketing tactics in Eastern Europe mirror those from the West: Eastern European dog lovers are therefore tempted to spend money on products with luxury-connoting exotic ingredients (lamb, bison, ostrich, salmon) or on ones promising to meet the needs of a specific group of dogs (e.g., foods for canine juniors, seniors, active dogs, giant breeds, overweight dogs). In addition to dry dog foods, a large selection of moist foods is also available, as well as a wealth of treats, pressed rawhide "bones," pigs' ears, rabbits' ears, and the like. Even the alternative to ready-made foods, home-prepared food, is becoming commercialized. The Biologically Appropriate Raw Foods (BARF) diet, based mostly on meat and bones, can serve as an example: In the second decade of the 21st century there are already several companies in Poland alone offering frozen, packed, and preportioned BARF products. Expensive diet supplements for dogs, such as salmon oil, are also readily available.

It should come to no surprise that the market of products for dogs reflects a society's more general consumer trends. The rise of hypermarkets, supermarkets, and shopping malls in the 1990s and 2000s was reflected by the demise of many round-the-corner grocery stores in major Polish cities. A similar fate awaited many family-run pet stores, now replaced by chains such as Kakadu and its 38 stores across the country. Aggressive advertisements of pet products attempt to convince dog guardians that the human-canine relationship goes significantly beyond eating scraps and cuddling. In a consumer-oriented free market economy, love and devotion can—and should—be expressed through the buying of proper accessories and gadgets, particularly those geared toward improving canine health (nutritional supplements) and safety (reflective collars, pet carriers, protective booties, canine seat belts, flea and tick preventatives), but also those that satisfy the dog's natural needs while its guardian is away or cannot interact with the dog (so-called educational toys). Furthermore, canine products reflect broader social changes and the reestablishment of the middle class; recently, alongside Poles' growing environmental awareness, eco-friendly and/or organic products for dogs emerged. Biodegradable pet waste bags and toys made of recycled materials, as well as handmade imperfect-but-one-of-a-kind accessories, are now readily available, although not surprisingly at a higher price.

The service sector also responds to emerging, often new, market demands. The last decade in Poland has witnessed the emergence of plentiful dog training schools—many (at least outwardly) advocating the use of state-of-the-art positive training methods—where canine guardians can undergo basic obedience training with their dogs but also train them in more specialized pursuits (for example, participating in canine performance sports and dog shows but also solving specific behavioral issues or phobias). Training philosophy has also undergone substantial changes, which are explored in detail in this book. In the second decade of the 21st century canine behaviorists—many of whom are excellent professionals constantly striving to improve their qualifications—offer their services to Poles in most of the bigger cities, as do groomers and dog walkers. Doggy daycare centers, and a range of dog boarding options, are also available. Last but not least, Polish dog lovers can choose to lay their beloved and departed canine friends to rest on the grounds of pet cemeteries, a concept born in 1991 and unavailable in Poland during communism.

The range of services for canines and their people is therefore already vast, but it is constantly growing as well. True to the logic of capitalism, all that is needed now is money. It is significant that the marketing of products and services for companion animals—like those for children—is, to a large extent, based on evoking feelings of guilt. The modern Pole's dog is his best friend or even a family member, and as such deserves the best.

The best is always expensive but how could one be stingy when it comes to the well-being of his or her loved ones…?[4]

It should be emphasized that contemporary veterinary medicine is in a similar predicament in that it is also governed by the "invisible hand" of the market. Recent advances in vet med open up treatment and rehabilitation possibilities previously unheard of in Poland (and elsewhere), but these are not available for everyone. Even though the costs of veterinary care are significantly lower in Poland than in the United States, so is the average wage. Sophisticated veterinary treatments are readily available for Polish canines and other species, but—again—cost accordingly. Unsurprisingly, the Polish public health-care system does not include four-legged friends and family members, so if a dog is hit by a car and requires surgeries and rehabilitation, the costs can add up quickly.

Cue the emergence of pet insurance, one of the newest products on the Polish market. Around 2005, PZU S.A., the leading insurance company in Poland, started offering a companion-animal-oriented product, *Cztery Łapy* (Four Paws), but it was discontinued in 2012, suggesting an unsatisfactory turnout and low public interest.[5] However, as of 2015, Poles can choose between at least two independent policies, offered by significantly lesser known companies, GasanMamo Insurance Ltd. and mySafety (*Gazeta Wyborcza*, 2014).[6] By purchasing pet insurance one can expect not only to obtain reimbursement in case of veterinary expenses but also to be compensated for the death of his or her beloved animal. Also included in the fee is a funeral allowance that facilitates the organization of a burial at a pet cemetery. The popularity of pet insurance seems to be a thing of the future, though, considering that the leading insurance companies in Poland have yet to offer (or, in case of PZU, reintroduce) their own companion animal products.

When Marley Replaced Szarik

The fascination of Poles with Western cultural patterns, as well as the effects of the globalization of consumer trends, is also reflected in the changes in the popularity of particular dog breeds. Analyzing breed preferences before and after 1989 allows us to observe a decrease in the popularity of protection dogs such as Giant Schnauzers, Dobermans, and Boxers.[7] Other breeds that fell out of favor include Poodles and Dachshunds, some of the most popular purebred dogs in the People's Republic of Poland. The latter were, in fact, something of a phenomenon—the perfect companions for apartment-dwellers in communist Poland, Dachshunds did not need much space (postwar Poland was notorious for housing shortages) and did not require much food. Communist Poland's love of Dachshunds culminated in the establishment in 1973 of an annual Dachshund parade. Curiously, the authorities barely tolerated the event, choosing to interpret it as a parody of the compulsory International Workers' Day parades on May 1 (Dachshund News, 2010).[8]

Nowadays an explosion of interest in a few types of breeds can be noted. Labrador Retrievers and Golden Retrievers, as well as British and American sheepdogs (Border Collies, Australian Shepherds) and small companion dogs (West Highland White Terriers, Yorkshire Terriers, Chinese Crested Dogs, and Chihuahuas) are among the most popular breeds in Poland. The Chihuahua's case is particularly striking, as the breed went from virtual absence up until the mid-1990s to being the most popular breed exhibited at the key international Polish dog show within a span of roughly 15 years.

These changes reflect the availability of pop-cultural models and their globalization: It is Hollywood—with the movies *Beverly Hills Chihuahua, Legally Blonde,* and *Marley and Me*—that now has a stronger influence on Polish dog breed preferences than the Polish television series *Four Tank-Men and a Dog.* Coincidentally, most of the breeds listed above (though not the Chihuahua) originate from Anglo-Saxon culture and their popularity is part and parcel of Poles' fascination with Anglo-Saxon countries and the sudden availability of British and American popular culture.

The fascination with Golden Retrievers and Labradors, the beginning of which coincides with the systemic transformation (these breeds were completely unknown in the communist Poland), also points to changes in Poles' understanding of the role of dogs in daily life. Twenty-five years ago the primary motivation for buying a large purebred dog was the dog's value as a potential guardian of one's property: a defender or hunter. The breeds that have gained popularity in the past two decades are mostly gentle and sociable dogs, advertised as ideal companions for children and good buddies for outdoor pursuits.[9] If a dog is to be large, then it should be a gentle giant, such as the Bernese Mountain Dog (with its popularity leap from virtual absence during communism to a top 10 ranking these days) or the Newfoundland. While Aaron Skabelund (2008, 2014) argued that the German Shepherd in films represented, in different geographic contexts, the spread of colonial rule through force and violence, the case of the real world popularity of the goofy Labrador from *Marley and Me* can be read as revealing how colonization can work through subtler and less violent means. In the Polish context, having a large-sized family dog such as a Labrador can be seen as the epitome of middle-class aspiration: the dog metonymically connotes a happy and affluent family life in a modern suburban or urban setting.

James Serpell, in his by now classic book *In the Company of Animals* (one of a few seminal animal studies works translated into Polish), described his own research in the United States concerning the expectations dog guardians have for their animals. According to his conclusions, those who are not looking for a working dog (that is, who do not need their dog to herd their flock of sheep, detect drugs, or pursue criminals) have mostly similar expectations of different breeds of dogs. They look for a dog who will want to form a close bond with them and, at the same time, who will not be aggressive or hyperactive (Serpell, 1986; cf. Chadwick, 2013). The expectations are, therefore, rather superficial and—as more recent research results by Stefano Ghirlanda, Alberto Acerbi, Hal Herzog, and Serpell (2013) confirm—do not necessarily match the characteristics and specificity of individual breeds. What they do reflect are fads and fashions, often motivated by popular culture. Individual preferences in regard to dogs are mostly aesthetic and include size, coat length and color, ear shape, and so forth. It is clear that breed preferences are culturally constructed, and the case of Poland after 1989 serves as yet another argument confirming this theory.

Writing about breeds, it is impossible to omit the *Związek Kynologiczny w Polsce* (Polish Kennel Club), the major organization supervising the breeding of purebred dogs in Poland. It was founded in 1938 as the English-sounding *Polski Kennel Club* then resurrected after World War II in 1948 under the more Polish-sounding name of *Związek Kynologiczny w Polsce*. The contemporary Polish Kennel Club is an association that aims to "promote the breeding and training of purebred dogs on the basis of scientific knowledge, in order to achieve the highest level of both conformation and utility" (Statut Związku Kynologicznego w Polsce, 2013). Throughout the decades of communism it was the only purebred dog registry in Poland and, therefore, the official one, organized in a way that reflected the structure of the Polish United Workers' Party apparatus: with a central and regional committees.

Unfortunately the Polish Kennel Club has not adapted well to the new reality, as both its structure and style of management remain a remnant of a bygone era. For example, it has been very slow in adapting solutions related to the welfare of dogs. Although anti-docking legislation has been in place in Poland since 1997[10] (albeit the phrasing of the legislation left room for unclear interpretations), the Polish Kennel Club did not ban the registration or showing of dogs with cropped ears and docked tails until 2011. The latter happened only after the wording of the law was clarified in a way that explicitly defined tail docking as a cosmetic procedure. The Polish Kennel Club was also very slow in implementing mandatory DNA testing (2015, though still only for breeding stock) and allowing microchipping as a permanent identification alternative to tattooing (2011).

Despite the Polish Kennel Club's explicit mission to combine conformation and utility, the organization seems to place much more emphasis on "beauty": the most popular activity supervised by the Club is dog shows. This state of affairs can also be discerned in the marginal role of the Polish Kennel Club in the popularization of so-called new canine performance sports. In fact, some of the noticeably flourishing canine-related activities in contemporary Poland are the ones not connected to the Club: canine disc (also known as dogfrisbee), flyball, rally obedience, mushing, and dogtrekking. These sports are organized by independent associations, often established by individuals frustrated with the lack of interest expressed by official authorities. Competitors in canine sports that operate under the auspices of the Polish Kennel Club are widely voicing their dissatisfaction with the undemocratic principles that seem to persistently govern the organization; for example, in 2014 Polish dog obedience competitors submitted a petition to the European umbrella organization, *Fédération Cynologique*

Internationale, complaining about unclear regulations and inconsistent judging criteria.[11] The petition was signed by 399 obedience enthusiasts.

Interestingly, other purebred dog registries, not affiliated with Polish Kennel Club, began mushrooming only after the Polish Parliament in 2011 (in force since January 1, 2012) voted in favor of an amendment to the 1997 Polish Animal Protection Act. Said amendment delegalized the breeding of cats and dogs "for commercial purposes" (Animal Protection Act of 1997, Art. 10a, item 2) with the exception of "breeders registered in nationwide breeding registries" (Animal Protection Act of 1997, Art. 10a, item 6). The changes were supposed to prevent the existence of puppy mills, where animals are bred without any kind of external supervision and where brood bitches are often in poor physical condition. However, the new law is an excellent example of legislation that has backfired, as it opened up the possibility for the registration of numerous shady organizations that claim to be breeding registries and that, in reality, simply issue "pedigrees" to any dog whose owner is willing to pay the registration fee. Poland's lesson appears to be as clear as it is unsurprising: legal actions can be helpful, but they cannot replace societal education.

The Shelter Business

Activities to reduce the population of homeless companion animals visibly intensified after 1989—on both the governmental and legislative levels, as well as through grassroots initiatives. A trend of promoting crossbred dogs as faithful companion animals has also become noticeable in the last few years. The 1997 Polish Animal Protection Act clearly states that an animal is not an object and firmly places the obligation of caring for homeless animals on the state's shoulders. Most Polish animal shelters are therefore funded with taxpayers' money and their work is overseen by local governments, predominantly by municipalities and rural communes, around the country.

The legislation, however, is far from perfect and, subsequently, the reality is far from rosy. As the *Fundacja dla Zwierząt "Argos"* (Foundation for Animals "Argos") explains, the 1997 Act defined the tasks of local government as "providing care for" and "catching" stray animals (predominantly dogs); however, only the latter term, *catching,* was further defined and discussed in detail by the implementation rules (Wypych, 2013). What the law has achieved is the clearing of stray dogs from city streets by reintroducing the profession of dogcatching. What it has not achieved, though, is improved conditions in shelters and increased adoption rates.

Polish animal shelters are, in general, expected to provide some care for the animals, but formally speaking there is no legal point of reference as to what "care" means and what it should entail (cf. Sowa, 2014; Wypych, 2013). Consequently, Polish shelters are notorious for overcrowding and for their overall struggle with ensuring animal welfare. Scandals related to poor management of animal shelters occasionally make even the national headlines, and some facilities have been accused of profiting from the misfortune of animals. One of the well-covered cases concerned Wojtyszki, a shelter in a rural area of central Poland eventually likened to a concentration camp. An esteemed weekly publication, *Polityka,* in a 2011 article with the telling title *"Fabryka psów"* (A dog factory), described the dogs of Wojtyszki in the following words:

> They get their food. There are no visible wounds, skin lesions, no pus in their eyes. Perhaps they do not get overly cold in the winter and do not suffer during sweltering heat. However, they will never, throughout their entire life in Wojtyszki, leave their runs, and the only human contact they get—excluding the whip—is a few minutes per day, when the caretaker unloads the food and cleans up their feces.
>
> None of them have a name. They are only microchip numbers. (Sowa, 2011)

According to the local district veterinary officer, in 2010 Wojtyszki housed a total of 2,372 dogs with only 19 adoptions recorded in that year. In 2013 the number of adoption rose to 339, but the number of dogs in the shelter increased nonetheless to 3,231 (Stowarzyszenie Obrona Zwierząt, 2013). Some of the runs in which the dogs are kept house approximately 100 dogs each.

Unfortunately, stories such as this one should not be surprising, considering that the funding shelters receive from their local government is legally tied to the number of admitted dogs and cats, instead of their subsequent living conditions or the number of adoptions performed by the shelter. Furthermore, local authorities are often passive (to say the least). When in 2013 the Supreme Audit Office of Poland controlled 18 municipalities to learn about their cooperation with local dogcatchers, it turned out that half of the authorities never followed up on the catching—that is, they never checked to confirm whether the animals were actually delivered to the shelter. More than 60 percent of the institutions did not set any animal welfare–related conditions in their contracts with either dogcatchers or shelters, whereas more than 80 percent did not require any form of record-keeping throughout the process (Siedlecka, 2013). This explains why it is very difficult to present all-encompassing, reliable, quantitative data regarding Polish shelters, their dwellers, and adoption rates. Unfortunately, the lack of reliable records and no pressure to create them facilitate the most shocking of the abuses, such as when animal shelter residents mysteriously disappear or when the most depraved and arrogant shelter personnel and dogcatchers play the catch-and-release game in order to be paid twice for the same animal (cf. Podgórska, 2011).

There is little doubt that the Wojtyszki shelter, with its growing numbers of dogs—and dogs per pen ratio—can be considered a dishonest enterprise. At the same time, it can also be seen as an example of animal welfare philosophy *à rebours*. Not only does Polish law struggle to define "providing care for" stray animals in shelters, it also largely ignores the subject of euthanization. By that logic, most Polish shelters—including Wojtyszki—can be considered "no-kill," and some of them actively take pride in that label, even when the adoption rates are not inspiring. A particularly glaring example comes from the Warsaw metropolitan area, where the well-known animal shelter Na Paluchu actually boasts on its website of being the largest animal shelter in the country "and maybe even in Europe," and provides an estimate of housing approximately 4,000 animals per year (ca. 2,300 dogs and 100 cats, as well as ferrets, rabbits, and other species).[12] In this context, knowledge that the largest animal shelters in Europe are presumably located in Poland takes on a sinister aspect, as does the awareness that the Polish Animal Protection Act does not point to adoption—or to anything else, for that matter—as the objective of keeping animals in shelters (Wypych, 2013).

In light of local authorities' lack of success in their operation of animal shelters, the role of grassroots organizations has increased in recent years. Some shelters, often the best ones, are operated by nonprofit organizations (predominantly foundations and associations), whose sustainability is not dependent upon government subsidies. The past two decades have also witnessed the establishment of groups (sometimes formalized as associations but sometimes completely informal) devoted to breed-specific rescue. Rescue organizations have been established for, among others, Rottweilers, Boxers, Border Collies, Alaskan Malamutes, and Golden Retrievers. A semiformal network of foster homes has also developed in the past 5 to 10 years: Volunteers temporarily bring homeless animals into their home and help with training and rehabilitation, while at the same time trying to find a suitable permanent home. It should come as no surprise that the concept of the animal foster home is also borrowed from Western Europe and the United States.

To the Rescue

Although formal research on the animal rescue community in Poland has yet to be conducted, even a brief look at Internet search results for animal rescue groups reveals that a great majority of the members of this community are female. This is likely because women are perceived as more emotionally sensitive than men and as having a greater sense of interdependence (cf. Gaarder, 2011; Herzog, 2007). The tabloid media sometimes misrepresent this female sensitivity, employing the figure of the "crazy lady" who cannot properly evaluate her capabilities, thus her desire to help strays backfires as she becomes unable to care for all of her animals. Unfortunately, there is some truth to this stereotype: the phenomenon is referred to as animal hoarding (cf. Arluke, 2006). Reports of organizations that intervene in such cases prove that, indeed, hoarders are mostly women, often older and single (Patronek, 1999). Animal hoarding can also affect those who are intensely involved in animal-related volunteer work; in some cases, pathological "collecting" of animals can suggest an existing psychological problem or a possible future one (Patronek, 1999). Animal hoarding has not been a significant problem in Poland—or at least has not been identified as one. However, the sensationalist vibe attracts the media.

One particular case received extensive media coverage, mostly because it pertained to a celebrity, the popular diva of yore, Violetta Villas. In the last years of her life, after her singing career was over, Villas attempted to help stray dogs and cats by taking them in, despite not having sufficient funds to cover their basic needs, not to mention her own. The story of Violetta Villas functions in the media as a warning about female sensitivity running wild, uncontrolled. The articles in the popular press repeatedly use such phrases as "she could not control herself," "she had no support," and "she could not handle it" (*Fakt,* 2011b; Podgórska, 2004).

Another recognizable and perhaps more disturbing case concerned Bożena Wahl, a painter and former director of a privately run animal shelter. Wahl, significantly lesser known than Villas but significantly more vocal, started a foundation to obtain financial support for her hundreds of dogs and a few dozen cats. In 2009, in light of dire animal welfare conditions, board members took over the foundation and removed Wahl. Public opinion was polarized, with many persons, unaware of hoarding as a disorder, expressing pity for the kind-hearted painter once informally dubbed "Mother Mary of Dogs" (Janiszewski, 2009). As of 2014 Wahl reportedly is again collecting stray animals (Białokoz, 2014).

Overcrowded shelters and hoarders' premises are worrisome, but where do all of the homeless dogs come from? Most of them are the result of society's carelessness and lack of knowledge related to canine reproduction. Here Poland is no different than many other Central, Southern, and Eastern European countries, although Polish streets, unlike those in Romanian, Russian, Bulgarian, and Ukrainian cities, are free from stray dogs because in Poland dogcatching is a profitable occupation. The news of thousands of stray dogs being caught and killed in Ukraine before the UEFA 2012 European Championship soccer games angered animal rights organizations, as did similar acts by Russian authorities before the 2014 Winter Olympic Games in Sochi. At the same time, stray dogs in cities have become associated with the recent urban protests in Greece (2008, 2011), and to the degree that a Wikipedia entry has been created for the term "riot dog."[13]

In Poland there is also a visible urban versus rural divide in approaches to canine welfare and reproduction: In the countryside dogs often run loose and no one interferes with their breeding. The myths that a neutered dog is somehow deficient and a bitch must have puppies at least once in her life, either for "health reasons" or "to experience the pleasures of motherhood," are commonplace. Puppy mill breeders also have their role in the overproduction of dogs. The puppies are often malnourished and raised in appalling conditions without any consideration for proper socialization. In effect, these puppies often end up suffering from behavioral and health issues as adult dogs.

The problem of commercial production of purebred dogs in Poland has not become a mass-scale issue as it has in the United States, where after World War II farmers were actually encouraged to switch from agricultural production to supplying puppies for the urban pet market (Grier, 2006, p. 351). The puppy mill model of animal breeding—opposed by many Americans—is one of the most obvious examples of the commodification of companion animals. The custom of offering dogs and cats for sale in pet shops never became widespread in Poland. It was unheard of in communist Poland and has been explicitly banned by the 2011 amendment to the Polish Animal Protection Act. For a time, it was common to find puppies offered for sale at livestock fairs and outdoor flea markets and in front of purebred dog shows. However, since the 2011 amendment took effect, this practice has been largely curtailed.

Strategies used to address the problem of stray animals in Poland are similar to those used in Western Europe. Many campaigns promoting the spaying and neutering of dogs (and cats) have been carried out in the past two decades, while the availability of these procedures has increased and their price has decreased. The nationwide campaign establishing March as a month when spay/neuter procedures are significantly discounted has been proving effective, based on the number of veterinary clinics that choose to join the program each year. There is also clear support of local governmental authorities for such campaigns. In 2015 the city of Warsaw introduced free spay/neuter procedures for animals whose guardians are residents of the city. However, nongovernmental organizations have been leading the field in popularizing the idea itself; in 2014 the *Fundacja Karuna* (Karuna Foundation) managed to involve some of the best-known Polish celebrities in a campaign that received impressive coverage in the media.

The popularity of spay/neuter procedures cannot improve the lives of the animals who are already in shelters, but in the long run it should most certainly decrease the number of shelter animals. Furthermore, while adoption rates still remain relatively low, it does seem that social consciousness related to homeless animals is changing, and Poles are not only becoming more aware of the need to solve this pressing issue but also beginning to put their money where their mouth is by donating increasingly more to charitable organizations. The weekly magazine *Polityka* claims that animal charities are the second largest source of Poles' donations to charities, after foundations aiding sick children (Ćwieluch, 2015).

It is also becoming a trend among Polish celebrities to care for mixed-breed and rescued dogs. Not only can one notice increased celebrity involvement in campaigns against cruelty and supporting spaying and neutering—the campaign organized by Karuna managed to attract the participation of three highly recognizable Polish actresses—but also celebrities are increasingly willing to be photographed on the covers of magazines with their own rescued pets. This trend is a reversal of the long association of social prestige with owning a purebred dog. Many researchers (cf. McHugh, 2004; Ritvo, 1987) argue that human aspirations of social advancement played a key role in the popularization of purebred dogs. However, Susan McHugh also notes that purebred dogs have become so widely available that they have ceased to serve as status symbols (McHugh, 2004, p. 103).

Poland seems to be slowly reaching this stage as well. "Soft values," those associated with emotions such as compassion and sympathy, have entered the public sphere, and this is why caring for a dog (particularly a rescue dog) now evokes positive emotions among one's constituents (for politicians) and fans (for media celebrities). While it is impossible to evaluate the genuineness of celebrities' affections for shelter dogs—in a society that values sensitivity to injustice, a public person's caring for a rescue dog can be an element of self-creation—it would be strategically inappropriate to criticize such trends in a country with overflowing animal shelters.

Mixed-breed dogs have also long been a symbol of nonconformity, rebellion, and disdain for mainstream social conventions, beauty standards, and racial purity. Writing about the United States, Susan McHugh (2004) notes that "by the twenty-first century, the mongrel dog has become a cross-cultural trope, a more literal underdog that is especially valuable for combatting the mechanisms of social oppression" (pp. 135–136). The case is no different in Poland: Mongrels are particularly popular among members of urban countercultures, such as feminists, anarchists, pacifists, and ecologists. For example, when one looks at the photographs of dogs attending Poland's largest feminist demonstration (organized in the capital city of Warsaw annually on March 8) taken by the author of the canine-themed blog *Pies w Warszawie* (Dog in Warsaw), it is difficult not to notice the predominance of mixed-breed dogs among the attendees.[14] It also speaks volumes that the blogger managed to photograph so many dogs at a political demonstration that overtly had nothing to do with improving animal welfare: It was about women's rights.

We opened this chapter by making the claim that since the reestablishment of democracy in 1989, being a dog guardian in Poland has become an important aspect of one's identity as a citizen; closing it with dogs attending a political demonstration with their people underscores this point.

Notes

1. Throughout the book, all translations from Polish to English are made by the editors, Michał Piotr Pręgowski and Justyna Włodarczyk, unless stated otherwise.
2. Comments in this paragraph pertaining to the published letter are from the online forum for the Warsaw supplement to *Gazeta Wyborcza.*
3. A notable exception was George Bush Senior's Springer Spaniel Millie, who not only had a litter of pups while in the White House but also "authored" (with the help of the First Lady) an autobiographical account of her life as America's First Dog. For an analysis of *Millie's Book,* see Colleen Glenney

Boggs' *Animalia Americana: Animal Representations and Biopolitical Subjectivity* (Columbia University Press, 2013).

4. It has become a common practice among members of closely knit Polish dogland communities (centered around involvement in a particular canine sport or dog shows, or fanciers of a particular breed) to organize fundraisers for dogs who require expensive treatment.
5. It is somewhat telling that at first pet insurance was available only within home insurance packages, wherein animals were recognized as possessions.
6. Other companies, such as Warta S.A., offer highly specialized products such as insurance policies for hunting dogs.
7. Regrettably, the Polish Kennel Club does not maintain full records concerning the number of registrations of purebred dogs and offers only partial and somewhat disorganized data. To observe trends in popularity we therefore chose to analyze official *Federation Cynologique International* show catalogs for Warsaw's annual International Dog Show from the 1990s to present. These catalogs contain full listings of all animals exhibited and, as such, constitute a valuable source of data about Poles' preferences. The following are a few examples from the catalogs of this popular Warsaw show held every July—Boxer: 46 dogs present at the show in 1998, 21 in 2012; Schnauzer (Giant and Standard): 66 in 1998, 19 in 2012; Chihuahuas: 0 in 1998, 92 in 2012; Border Collie: 1 in 1998, 24 in 2012; Labrador Retriever: 18 in 1998, 76 in 2012.
8. Agnieszka Kuczyńska, one of the organizers of the parade, explained to the *Daily Dachshund* in the September 7, 2010, article "Some History of the Krakow Dachshund Parade": "The first march was very unusual. The Sausage Dogs arrived at the parade in carriages and waiters served sausages on silver trays. It's true that the editor in chief of *Przekrój* magazine, Mieczysław Czuma, who initiated the event, could have faced serious consequences. He was held accountable for provoking the authorities and ridiculing the May 1st parade. Of course this was not his intention but in those days the authorities were not ready for this kind of event, so it was banned." Article available at http://dailydachshunddanddognews.com/some-history-of-the-krakow-dachshund-parade/ [Accessed 18 April 2015].
9. Of course, expectations are often not matched by the reality of interacting with a particular representative of a breed, especially if the expectations

were formed in response to pop-cultural representations. Many dog trainers are acutely aware of this, as they spend their time working with aggressive Golden Retrievers and phonophobic Border Collies.

10. Article 27 of the Animal Protection Act of 1997.
11. "Discrimination of Polish Competitors Has to Stop!": https://www.change.org/p/fci-f%C3%A9d%C3%A9ration-cynologique-internationale-discrimination-of-polish-competitors-has-to-stop-stanowczy-sprzeciw-wobec-dyskryminacji-polskich-zawodnik%C3%B3w-obedience-przez-zkwp [Accessed 15 April 2015].
12. Data provided on the shelter's website: http://www.paluch.org.pl/index.php?do=history&what=3 [Accessed 13 April 2015].
13. See http://en.wikipedia.org/wiki/Riot_dog [Accessed 17 April 2015].
14. Pies w Warszawie, *Fotorelacja: Manifa, marzec, 2012*, entry dated March 11, 2012, http://pieswwarszawie.blogspot.com/2012/03/fotorelacje-manifa-marzec-2012.html [Accessed 11 November 2013]. In 2015 the blog was moved to a stand-alone address, www.pieswwarszawie.pl, and the Blogspot archives are no longer accessible.

References

Animal Protection Act of 1997. (1997, September 23). Retrieved from Internetowy System Aktów Prawnych [Internet Legal Acts Repository], http://isip.sejm.gov.pl/DetailsServlet?id=WDU19971110724 [Accessed 11 January 2016].

Arluke, A. (2006). *Just a dog: Understanding animal cruelty and ourselves.* Philadelphia, PA; Temple University Press.

Atkins, P. (Ed.). (2012). *Animal cities: Beastly urban histories.* Aldershot, UK: Ashgate Publishing, Ltd.

Baker, S. (2000). *Postmodern animal.* London, UK: Reaktion Books.

Białokoz, N. (2014). Nałogowi zbieracze psów. Miłość bez happy endu [Dog hoarders: Love without a happy ending]. *Pies, 10.* Retrieved from http://www.pies.pl/temat-miesiaca-nalogowi-zbieracze-psow/ [Accessed 11 January 2016].

Bulliet, R. W. (2005). *Hunters, herders, and hamburgers: The past and future of human-animal relationships.* New York, NY: Columbia University Press.

Chadwick, D. (2013). Why "pure breed" dogs can't fetch: An interview with James Serpell. *Stay Free, 22.* Retrieved from http://www.stayfreemagazine.org/archives/22/james-serpell-dog-breeding.html [Accessed 23 May 2015].

Ćwieluch, J. (2015). Jeden procent, dziesięć zmartwień [One percent, ten worries]. *Polityka, 16* (3005), 22–25.

Dachshund News. (2010). Some history of the Krakow Dachshund parade. Retrieved from http://dailydachshundanddognews.com/some-history-of-the-krakow-dachshund-parade [Accessed 23 May 2015].

Derr, M. (2004). *A dog's history of America: How our best friend explored, conquered, and settled a continent.* New York, NY: North Point Press.

Fakt. (2010, April 23). Zwierzęta prezydenta znalazły nowy dom [Presidential animals have found a new home]. *Fakt.* Retrieved from http://www.fakt.pl/Zwierzeta-prezydenta-znalazly-nowy-dom,artykuly,70042,1.html [Accessed 23 May 2015].

Fakt. (2011a, September 12). To ona tak naprawdę rządzi w Belwederze! [The true top dog at Belvedere!]. *Fakt.* Retrieved from http://www.fakt.pl/To-ona-tak-naprawde-rzadzi-w-Belwederze-,artykuly,114525,1.html [Accessed 23 May 2015].

Fakt. (2011b, December 2011). Violetta Villas i Zwierzęta. Tak je kochała! [Violetta Villas and animals: She loved them so!]. *Fakt.* Retrieved from http://www.fakt.pl/Violetta-Villas-i-zwierzeta-Tak-je-kochala-,artykuly,138950,1.html [Accessed 23 May 2015].

Franklin, A. (1999). *Animals and modern cultures: A sociology of human-animal relations in modernity.* London, UK: Sage Publications.

Gaarder, E. (2011). *Women and the animal rights movement.* New Brunswick, NJ: Rutgers University Press.

Gazeta Wyborcza. (2014, January 3). Miliardy na psy i koty. Karma to za mało. Spa, DogTV i polisa na leczenie [Billions spent on dogs and cats: With spa, DogTV and pet insurance, the food is just the beginning]. Retrieved from http://wyborcza.biz/biznes/1,101562,15220178,Miliardy_na_psy_i_koty__Karma_to_za_malo__Spa__DogTV.html [Accessed 11 January 2016].

Gazeta Wyborcza Stołeczna. (2013, July 31). Ja i mój pies czujemy się wykluczeni [My dog and I feel excluded]. Retrieved from http://warszawa.gazeta.pl/warszawa/1,34862,14361382,Wlascicielka_psa__Ja_i_moj_pies_czujemy_sie_wykluczeni.html [Accessed 23 May 2015].

Ghirlanda, S., Acerbi, A., Herzog, H., & Serpell, J. (2013). Fashion vs. function in cultural evolution: The case of dog breed popularity. *PLoS ONE, 8*(9), e74770. http://dx.doi.org/10.1371/journal.pone.0074770

Grier, K. C. (2006). *Pets in America: A history.* Chapel Hill: University of North Carolina Press.

Haraway, D. (2008). *When species meet.* Minneapolis: University of Minnesota Press.

Herzog, H. (2007). Gender differences in human–animal interactions: A review. *Anthrozoos, 20*(1), 7–21. http://dx.doi.org/10.2752/089279307780216687

Herzog, H. (2010). *Some we love, some we hate, some we eat: Why it's so hard to think straight about animals.* New York, NY: HarperCollins.

Hunter, J. D. (1992). *Culture wars: The struggle to control the family, art, education, law, and politics in America.* New York, NY: Basic Books.

Janiszewski, B. (2009). Upadek psiej mamy [The fall of the dog mother]. *Newsweek Polska,* 37/2009.

Koch-Kostersitz, M. (1988). *400 rad dla miłośników psów* [400 tips for dog lovers] (J. Grabowski, Trans. from German). Warsaw, Poland: Państwowy Instytut Wydawniczy.

Konecki, K. (2005). *Ludzie i ich zwierzęta. Interakcjonistyczno—symboliczna analiza społecznego* świata *właścicieli zwierząt domowych* [People and their animals: An interactionist-symbolic analysis of the social world of companion animal owners]. Warsaw, Poland: Scholar.

Lipiński, P. (2014, May 7). Tak wyglądał dzień, w którym po raz pierwszy ukazała się "Wyborcza" [This is what the day when Wyborcza was first published looked like]. *Gazeta Wyborcza.* Retrieved from http://wyborcza.pl/1,138142,15914945,Orgazm_z_przydzialu__Tak_wygladal_dzien__w_ktorym.html [Accessed 23 May 2015].

Marcus, G. E. (2002). *Sentimental citizen: Emotion in democratic politics.* University Park, PA: Penn State University Press.

McHugh, S. (2004). *Dog.* London, UK: Reaktion Books.

Novek, J. (2005). Pigs and people: Sociological perspectives on the discipline of nonhuman animals in intensive confinement. *Society & Animals, 13*(3), 221–244. http://dx.doi.org/10.1163/1568530054927771

Patronek, G. (1999). Hoarding of animals: An under-recognized public health problem in a difficult-to-study population. *Public Health Reports, 114*(1–2)/ 1999, 81–87. http://dx.doi.org/10.1093/phr/114.1.81

Piątek, M. (2015). Okupowani [Occupied]. *Polityka, 16*(3005)/2015.

Piotrowska, E. (2014). *A ja jestem Polak mały, moim krajem jest* świat *cały* [I am a little Pole, the whole world is my home]. Warsaw, Poland: Czarna Owca.

Podgórska, J. (2004). Gumowce dla Kopciuszka [Wellingtons for Cinderella]. *Polityka, 36*(2468)/2004.

Podgórska, J. (2011). Pieskie życie, pieska śmierć [A dog's life, a dog's death]. *Polityka, 10*(2797)/2011.

Rappaport, H. (2003). *Queen Victoria: A biographical companion.* Santa Barbara, CA: ABC-CLIO.

Ritvo, H. (1987). *The animal estate: The English and other creatures in the Victorian Age.* Cambridge, MA: Harvard University Press.

Ritvo, H. (2007). On the animal turn. *Daedalus, 136*(4), 118–122. http://dx.doi .org/10.1162/daed.2007.136.4.118

Serpell, J. (1986). *In the company of animals.* Oxford, UK: Basil Blackwell.

Shukin, N. (2009). *Animal capital: Rendering life in biopolitical times.* Minneapolis: University of Minnesota Press.

Siedlecka, E. (2013, August 5). Jak gminy pozbywają się bezdomnych zwierząt—wstrząsający raport NIK [How municipalities get rid of the homeless animals: A shocking report by the Supreme Audit Office]. *Gazeta Wyborcza.* Retrieved from http://wyborcza.pl/1,76842,14387208,Jak_gminy _pozbywaja_sie_bezdomnych_zwierzat___wstrzasajacy.html [Accessed 23 May 2015].

Skabelund, A. (2008). Breeding racism: The imperial battlefields of the "German" Shepherd dog. *Society & Animals, 16*(4), 354–371. http://dx.doi.org/10.1163 /156853008X357676

Skabelund, A. (2014). Dogs at war: Military dogs in film. In A. L. McLean (ed.), *Cinematic canines: Dogs and their work in the fiction film* (pp. 123–142). New Brunswick, NJ: Rutgers University Press.

Sowa, A. (2011). Fabryka psów [A dog factory]. *Polityka, 33*(2820)/2011.

Sowa, A. (2014). Doktor Hycel [Doctor dogcatcher]. *Polityka, 11*(2949)/2014.

Statut Związku Kynologicznego w Polsce. Rozdział II, § 6. [Statute of the Polish Kennel Club, Chapter II, § 6]. (2013). Retrieved from http://www.zkwp.pl /zg/regulaminy/Statut_ZKwP.pdf [Accessed 12 October 2013].

Stowarzyszenie Obrona Zwierząt [Association for the Defense of Animals]. (2013). Obóz koncentracyjny Wojtyszki [Wojtyszki concentration camp]. Retrieved from http://www.obrona-zwierzat.pl/wojtyszki.html [Accessed 13 April 2015].

Super Express. (2010, February 2). Jakiego pieska chcesz w Pałacu Prezydenckim? Lulę czy Drakę? [Which doggie would you like to see in the presidential palace? Lula or Draka?]. *Super Express.* Retrieved from http://www.se.pl/wydarzenia/kraj/jakiego-pieska-chcesz-w-paacu-lule-czy-drake_131317.html [Accessed 23 May 2015].

Super Express. (2011, May 6). Draka—prezydencki pies przywitał Królową Szwecji Sylwię [Draka—President's dog greets Sylvia the Queen of Sweden]. *Super Express.* Retrieved from http://www.se.pl/wydarzenia/kraj/draka-prezydencki-pies-przywital-krolowa-szwecji-sylwie_183679.html [Accessed 23 May 2015].

Weil, K. (2010). A report on the animal turn. *Differences: A Journal of Feminist Cultural Studies, 21*(2), 1–23. http://dx.doi.org/10.1215/10407391-2010-001

Wypych, T. (2013). Hyclostwo [Dogcatching]. *Inwestycje Sektora Publicznego,* April–June 2013.

2

Toward Mutual Understanding, Respect, and Trust: On Past and Present Dog Training in Poland

Agnieszka Orłowska

The history of dog training in Poland is neither very long, nor particularly exceptional. Of course, some forms of taking advantage of and shaping of canines' instinctive behaviors—particularly hunting and guarding homesteads and flocks of livestock—have a long tradition in Poland, but dog training as a popular and organized activity based on a coherent methodology, recorded in written sources that can serve as the subject of systematic analysis, first appeared only in the early 20th century. The methods applied by Polish trainers, during the period discussed here (1950s–2010), were influenced by the availability of training literature in Polish (sometimes, a training philosophy became popular after a translation of a particular training book had been published in Polish), the charisma and media presence of training authorities, the influence of technology (particularly the Internet), and general trends in Poles' attitudes toward companion animals. Most significantly, after 1989 there slowly begins to appear increased interest in methods based on positive reinforcement and the concurrent turn to emotional-cognitive education (which hereafter I refer to as upbringing). It cannot be denied that these changes were somewhat delayed, as compared to trends in Western Europe,

North America, and Australia; however, their very appearance can be correlated in time with Poland opening itself to the West in the last decade of the 20th century.

This chapter is written from the perspective of a practitioner—someone who has been an active dog trainer for several decades and has had the opportunity to observe firsthand the changes in the methods of dog training in Poland and the reactions to these changes. My goal is to outline the general directions of the transformation, as well as to point out the existence of its contestation. Irrational opposition to change and the persistence of outdated and clearly ineffective methods were the obstacles which the precursors of new training methods had to face.

Cynagogy

Terms such as *education, upbringing, teaching,* and *training* are defined differently, and in ways that are often contradictory. All of these terms are within the field of interest of pedagogy. The word *pedagogy* comes from the Greek *paidagogos* (literally, "leading the child"), and it was initially used to describe childcare, child-rearing, upbringing, and, finally, the formal education of children and youth. More recently, the education of adults has begun to be referred to as *andragogy,* a branch of pedagogy (cf. Knowles, 1968; Merriam, 2001). This chapter carries out a somewhat daring extrapolation and introduces the concepts of education, upbringing, and teaching into the sphere of cynagogy,[1] as this will make it easier to trace and understand the changes taking place in the methods of working with dogs over the past several decades and the evolution of the human-canine bond in Poland.

For the purposes of this chapter, I have adopted the classification proposed by Bolesław Niemierko (2007), a well-known Polish theorist of education, who assumes that each educational activity comprises two aspects: the emotional-motivational aspect and the cognitive-intellectual aspect. The first aspect refers to emotions, motivations, desires, and involvement and the second aspect to knowledge, skills, and capacities of the students, in this case: the dog. Taking into account the significance of these aspects in the planning, implementation, and effects of educational activities, one can distinguish between (1) upbringing, (2) training, (3) teaching, and (4) education.

Following this classification by Niemierko, though it must be emphasized that Niemierko is writing about human students, one could define a dog's (1) upbringing (or: emotional education) as educational activities oriented at emotional changes and, indirectly, at cognitive changes (Niemierko, 2007, p. 35). The process of upbringing would result in the dog's capability of controlling his emotions and drives, in accordance with norms accepted both in the canine and human worlds. The entire process of a canine's socialization consists of the following elements: the development of the dog's ability to control his emotions; the building up of the dog's social competencies in contacts with others dogs and people; desensitization training and motivation-building, understood as developing a dog's natural predispositions; and the reinforcing of a dog's trust for the guardian. A dog who has been well brought up—in other words, a dog whose process of upbringing has been successful—is a dog who is not shy, who is confident, exhibits self-control, is open to his environment, is willing to enter into relationships with people and other dogs, is trusting toward his guardian, and is willing to cooperate with humans.

According to Niemierko, (2) training (or: cognitive education) can be defined as educational activities oriented at achieving cognitive changes and indirectly at emotional changes. The results of training would include the acquisition of knowledge and skills necessary for achieving cognitive and practical goals (Niemierko, 2007, pp. 35–36). One could say that in the case of cynagogy, activities such as competitive obedience training and utility training can be seen as a direct part of training because the aim of these activities is to equip the dog with specific skills: the ability to perform certain behaviors on cue. A high level of training is seen as a necessary element for preparing dogs to work with humans and to undertake the various tasks humans expect dogs to perform for them.

Meanwhile (3) teaching (or: emotional-cognitive education) can be defined as educational activities balanced in their emotional-motivational aspects and cognitive-intellectual aspects (Niemierko, 2007, p. 36). In this context, the effects of teaching could be described as the dog's ability to carry out tasks which have been entrusted to him and the ability to achieve goals deemed as significant by the dog. The skill of an animal's independent decision making—in a way which agrees with his nature and which is, at the same time, in accordance with what the human defines as correct; a decision enabling the successful completion of the task—is testimony to effective teaching.

According to Niemierko (2007), the last element, (4) education, pertains to all educational activities and is a term which contains within itself upbringing, teaching, and training. The term comes from the Latin *educare,* which was originally connected to the "bringing to light" or "bringing to the surface," which perfectly emphasizes the aspect of acknowledging and skillfully developing the individual's talents and predispositions (p. 36). These definitions are obviously somewhat simplified; however, they are useful for emphasizing the need to balance between the emotional and cognitive aspects of educational activities. Adopting this terminology from the field of pedagogy makes it easier to trace certain patterns in the evolution of dog training methods: the shift from upbringing to training and then the gradual (re)inclusion of teaching and upbringing in "canine education."

In the English-speaking world of dog lovers, the word *training* is seen as transparent: it is neutral and objective. While the methods may change, there is hardly any opposition to the label of training. It is in the field of pedagogy where the emotional charge of these vocabulary items becomes evident. When in 1994 Michael and Debi Pearl published a controversial childcare booked titled *To Train Up a Child,* scandal ensued. The title itself suggests that the book might advocate unusually strict methods. In the Polish language the word traditionally used to refer to dog training is *tresura,* a word used only in relation to the training of animals and etymologically close to the German *Dressur* and the French *dresser.* All the training books from the 1960s and 1970s discussed in this article use the term *tresura,* while the newer ones, associated with the changes in training methods that took place in the early 21st century, prefer the term *szkolenie,* which etymologically derives from the Latin *schola,* similarly to the English *school* (and the Polish equivalent *szkoła*), and which is associated with a comprehensive educational approach. The dog training revolution in Poland thus also had a linguistic dimension.

Beginnings of Canine Emotional Education (Upbringing)

Should one accept Raymond and Lorna Coppingers' theory of the natural selection that led to the domestication of wolves (Coppinger & Coppinger, 2001),[2] one could conclude that the genetic changes which were taking place during the process of domestication were an educational activity enabling the adaptation of these proto-dogs to a new, manmade environment.[3] Humans had very little participation in the process. Our ancestors' only achievement in the process of the domestication of wolves was the change in their lifestyle: By settling down, setting up villages, and throwing away refuse, they created a new niche. This niche provided easy access to food and subsequently increased reproductive opportunities while, in the long run, also increasing the chances of survival in the presence of humans. As Raymond Coppinger writes, proto-dogs were better garbage eaters than were wolves because they were less afraid of people—that is, their flight distance was significantly shorter.[4] They became genetically tame, in contrast to regular wolves with long flight distance. It was also more advantageous for proto-dogs to scavenge along the borders of human settlements and to closely monitor human activity, rather than avoid it. Thus, they followed humans and became increasingly closer to human dwellings (Coppinger & Coppinger, 2001, pp. 60–61).

When early dogs were living on the borders of settlements and dwellings, humans' relationship with them became commensal. The next stage, that is, dogs' entry into the human settlements, changed the relationship from commensality to mutuality. By becoming a part of the human social world, dogs began to serve people: they guarded and herded livestock, retrieved game, pulled sleds, and so forth. Coppinger doubts whether canines' motivation to serve humankind was simply driven by the possibility of being fed. In addition to other aspects, such gratification would have been too delayed in time. Coppinger concludes that dogs were not working simply to obtain a food reward (Coppinger & Coppinger, 2001, pp. 97–100).

Ever since dogs began to live among people and work for them, they also started to be socialized in the human environment and the imprinting of social partners of another species commenced; the dogs' natural predispositions were developed and their trust in their guardians increased. At this point, the key elements of upbringing can be discerned.

At first humans were not interested in directing the breeding selection of dogs in relation to particular features, but with time, lack of breeding selection began to be replaced with artificial selection. Humans recognized the prized features of particular individuals and began to prefer—this still cannot be called conscious breeding selection—certain types of dogs. Long-nosed and long-legged dogs, resembling contemporary sight hounds, helped humans obtain food; dogs with the best sense of smell scented and tracked game; huge and big-headed dogs accompanied troops during military excursions, evoking fear among enemies. Large dogs could have also served as draft animals and smaller ones helped with pest control.

Civilizational progress also brought about the conscious development of dog breeding, focusing on increased specialization. The aristocracy's penchant for hunting led to the development of many breeds of hunting dogs, often suited to specific geographic localities, such as hounds, wolfhounds, bloodhounds, spaniels, and dogs used to hunt wild boars, foxes, otters, and so forth. While canines are currently valued mostly for their sociability, one should not forget that that the primary type of selection was connected to their genetic lack of fear of humans, connected to their abilities of scavenging and monitoring human activity.

The second stage of humans' journey in time with canines included a significant new factor: conscious breeding selection with regard to specific qualities. Humans' educational activities were still mostly restricted to the dogs' upbringing: taking advantage of natural instincts of some types of dogs, which were consciously selected for. The desired instincts were reinforced and others were tempered. Elements of training also appeared—for example the punishing of strong-willed dogs; the use of praise and food as rewards; adjusting training to suit the animal's temperament. However, these activities were still isolated and did not create the foundations for what could be termed as a consistent dog training methodology.

Beginnings of Cognitive Education (Training)

Civilizational progress left many dogs "unemployed," but new opportunities opened up for canines in the early 20th century: work in the uniformed professions. The sources of activities aimed at cognitive changes can be located in publications from this period. This is when dog training truly begins. The first modern dog training methods were prepared for the purposes of the military and police forces, and the German police officer, Konrad Most, was a pioneer in this field. In *Die Abrichtung des Hundes* (Dog training: A manual), the dog training handbook he published in 1910, Most emphasizes the role of instinct and hunting drive in obtaining desired behaviors; he advocates both the use of force and encouragement; he distinguishes between conditional and unconditional stimuli; he presents a method of shaping behaviors; and he points out the significance of synchronizing in time the reward or punishment with the behavior.

In other words, Most understood the basic features of operant conditioning almost 30 years before these were officially published by Burrhus F. Skinner (1938) in *The Behavior of Organisms.* Many followers of Konrad Most soon appeared worldwide, and his training philosophy became hugely popular and still remains foundational for what is usually termed as "traditional" dog training. It consists mostly (although not only) of enforcing obedience through coercion; the training tools include a whip and a prong collar, and the human-canine relationship is unilateral and highly confrontational. In 1910 Konrad Most wrote:

> Even the most soft-hearted dog-owner cannot get on terms with his idolized favorite without some form of compulsion. In the absence of compulsion neither human education nor canine training is feasible. (Most, 1910/2000, p. 27)

> As in a pack of dogs, the order of hierarchy in a man and dog combination can only be established by physical force, that is, by an actual struggle, in which the man is instantly victorious. Such a result can only be brought about by convincing the dog of the absolute physical superiority of the man. Otherwise the dog will lead and the man follow. If a dog shows the slightest sign of rebellion against his trainer or leader, the physical superiority of the man as leader of the pack must be given instant expression in the most unmistakable manner. Should a dog rebel against his trainer, instant resort to severe compulsion is essential. (Most, 1910/2000, p. 35)

This archaic and simplistic emphasis on a dog's submission and total obedience, obtained through the use of compulsion and physical force, is still to be found on bookstore shelves in contemporary Poland, particularly in translations of best-selling English language publications, which are popular among readers and criticized by scientific experts (cf. Millan & Peltier, 2007a, 2007b; Monks of New Skete, 1978).[5]

The best known proponent of Konrad Most's training methods in Poland was Colonel Antoni Brzezicha. Brzezicha had a military background and was the longtime chairman of the General Committee for Dog Training of the Polish Kennel Club and a trainer of police dogs. His first book, *Amatorskie szkolenie psów* (Amateur dog training), was initially published in 1973 and was reissued six times by 1989. Brzezicha's books were published through 2002. Konrad Most's ideas on compelling a dog to submit through the use of physical force are echoed by Brzezicha:

> The instinct of the untrained dog is full of freedom and liberty and this is why, in the beginning stages of training, he will react with resistance. The trainer's main task will thus be to break the dog's resistance and force him into submission and unconditional obedience. (Brzezicha, 1997, p. 7)

> It is often the case that some dogs do not submit to training. This happens when they detect the handler's [dog guardian's] weakness and indecisiveness. In such cases the animal tries to take over

> the leadership role, which, of course, precludes the possibility of further training unless the handler uses a strong, direct, mechanical stimulus, thus enforcing submission and obedience. (Brzezicha, 2002, p. 14)

Brzezicha was also a strong proponent of the now discredited (cf. Coppinger & Coppinger, 2001) yet still influential wolf pack model of human-canine coexistence:

> For the domestic dog, devoid of the company of other canines, the pack is somewhat replaced by the household members; in the dog's mind, there can only be one leader of this pack and this person becomes the dog's master, while the remaining household members are placed lower on the rungs of the ladder of pack hierarchy. (Brzezicha, 2002, p. 14)

Brzezicha's *Amatorskie szkolenie psów* was not, however, the only Polish dog training handbook. It was preceded by over a decade by Jan Gieżyński's *Amatorska tresura psów użytkowo-obronnych* (Amateur training of protection-utility dogs). Gieżyński was also a military person, an avid hunter, and the author of a popular hunting dog training book *Szkolenie psów myśliwskich* (Training hunting dogs [1964], reissued 13 times). Gieżyński assumes that the value of a good hunting or protection dog is connected primarily to the dog's upbringing and the careful developing of his natural predispositions in the period of early adolescence. Gieżyński was motivated to write his books by the almost total lack of dog training literature in postwar Poland. In addition to training protocols, his books also contained guidelines for "communicating with dogs," which can be interpreted as a turn toward mutuality in the human-canine relationship.

Gieżyński's strong emphasis on the importance of upbringing, basing the training process on the dog's natural predispositions and their skillful shaping, was not a common approach at the time. Gieżyński, known as Major by his friends, was, most definitely, ahead of his time: he pointed out the importance of gradual and planned socialization, warned about the dangers of overstimulating young puppies, saying that too much stimulation can be just as harmful as a completely non-stimulating environment. The period of a dog's upbringing should, according to Gieżyński, take place between 3 and 12 months of age, and it should consist of socialization, defined by the author as "gradually familiarizing the pup with all possible phenomena that he may encounter later on in life," the development of the pup's physical prowess, the gradual development of responses that will facilitate future training, and the shaping of a type of dog that will exhibit proper drives (Gieżyński, 1958, p. 37). There are no traces of the struggle for leadership in the pack, no signs of "breaking" the dog or fighting for the alpha position in Gieżyński's book.

Formal teaching, which according to Gieżyński (1958) should begin when a dog turns 12 months of age, was seen as the extension of upbringing, with emphasis on the development of inborn and acquired traits and their adjustment to suit the needs of the dog's guardian. Gieżyński discussed the training methods he was familiar with, dividing them into three main types: (1) compulsion-based: a type of training that he criticized for the distrust it built between the dog and the trainer and the likelihood of building up fear and possible fear-based aggression toward humans; (2) treat-based: a type of training that he recognized as strengthening advantageous responses, increasing the speed of a dog's learning process, and creating a strong bond between the dog and the trainer; however, Gieżyński also critically acknowledge the problems with competing motivation that could not be resolved through the use of this method (these included the presence of another dog or of game); and (3) contrast-based: a type of training which consisted of the combining of the first two types—that is, of rewarding tasks that were correctly performed and punishing the dogs for incorrect responses. Gieżyński saw the third method as the only basic method which brought about complete results. At the same time, he emphasized that

> compulsion should not be understood literally as physical pressure exerted upon the dog, but rather as an educational method which does not allow the dog complete freedom in his activities, yet one which facilitates the association that the dog's guardian can see

> everything, that he rewards correct responses and will not allow any slackening. This requires that the guardian carefully observe the dog's behavior, his manner of working; that he analyze the reasons for the dog's reactions and consider the possibilities of correcting mistakes. (Gieżyński, 1958, p. 47)

It should be mentioned that this progressive approach to working with dogs did not become popular among the practitioners of amateur dog training.

The methods of upbringing and training proposed by Lubomir Smyczyński, chairman of the Polish Association of Purebred and Working Dogs in the interwar period (1918–1939), later also a member of the scientific board of the Polish Kennel Club and an honorary member of the Club, met with a similar fate. Smyczyński was the author of the first book about dogs published after World War II in Poland, *Psy, rasy, hodowla, szkolenie* (Dogs, breeds, breeding, training [1948]; reissued multiple times). Smyczyński wished to familiarize his readers with the domestic dog and to provide answers to the question he found the most significant: How does one communicate with a dog? Smyczyński could thus be seen as a precursor to and advocate of mutuality in the human-canine relationship; the kind of mutuality which can later be recognized in Gieżyński's writings. Smyczyński asks the fundamental question: upbringing or training? (that is, educational activities directed at emotional changes or cognitive changes?). The author devotes an entire chapter to this issue and emphasizes that proper upbringing is the foundation of further teaching; he also does not shy away from analogizing human to canine education, stating that proper upbringing is necessary for both children and pups. While Gieżyński did look at the human-canine relationship through the perspective of the wolf pack, Smyczyński emphasized different aspects of pack life than did Konrad Most and his advocates:

> The handler's attitude toward the dog should be based on the principle of coexistence in a pack. The master should certainly have the authority to quell any rebellion, but he should also evoke boundless trust. The dog should know that he is safe next to his master,

> that together they form a team that can control the environment. (Smyczyński, 1948/1989, p. 43)

In the process of teaching, Smyczyński was an advocate of the maxim "teach by playing, learn by playing." He was certain of the effectiveness of his method, and he opposed other ways of training dogs:

> One should not be afraid that a dog who learns during play will be less effective at work. On the contrary, if his instincts have been properly developed and channeled through play into acceptable forms, he will exhibit obedience and willingness at work. His behavior will result from his inborn instincts which have been properly directed by the human. Experience shows that both punishment and compulsion as impeding factors are less effective than rewards and pleasant stimuli, in accordance with the dog's natural inclinations. (Smyczyński, 1948/1989, p. 43)

Unfortunately, the progressive attitudes of Smyczyński and Gieżyński were eclipsed in Poland by Brzezicha's military drilling and Most's "hard" theory of dominance. Why did this happen? It is difficult to answer with certainty. After becoming acquainted with the publications of all three authors, I was once fascinated with the false (something we were not aware of at the time) wolf pack model and with dominance, which consisted of enforcing submission and obedience, under the mistaken illusion that if I remained close to wolf/dog nature it would help me understand dogs better and help me speak their language. I justified the use of physical force in dog training with the rules of pack behavior and that is why I resorted to it. I suppose that many other dog trainers in the early 1990s behaved in a similar manner, even though they had a lot of respect and love for these animals.

For many years the "contrast method," which consisted of forcing the dog to perform a particular action through mechanical stimuli and then rewarding the dog for performing the action, was the most popular dog training technique in Poland. The force of the mechanical stimuli gradually decreased: prong collars were first replaced with choke collars and later with flat buckle collars. The use of reinforcement, particularly food rewards, increased; praise and pats were augmented with tasty morsels and play with the dog's guardian.[6]

It is virtually impossible to determine the first Polish trainer to reward a dog with a toy. However, it was most certainly a breakthrough moment for what became known as "training in drive," which became popular in the mid-1980s. The basic assumption of this method is to bring out and take advantage of a dog's natural hunting instincts—his desire to chase, grab, and kill game. This desire is redirected onto a tug toy, a ball, or some other artificial moving object, which the dog is encouraged to chase, grab, hold, and shake in his mouth. A dog with strong prey drive can become very involved in this game and can put a lot of effort into performing exercises correctly, only to obtain the desired object and to be able to play the game together with his trainer. While training through prey drive most certainly increases the dog's enthusiasm, the training methods, at least as they were applied in Poland in the 1980s and 1990s, did not include new ways of obtaining the desired behaviors. In other words, while the dog was rewarded with play, and the training session itself was fast-paced and exciting, he still had to be physically manipulated to assume the desired positions. Additionally, the dog's boundless enthusiasm had to be curbed before his performance was deemed precise enough to make him ready to participate in a trial, and this curbing took place with the use of corrections.

It should be added that while training through prey drive became popular among participants of protection dog trials, the most popular canine performance activity in Poland through the 1990s, it never achieved mainstream popularity among owners of pet dogs. Additionally, because this type of training relied to a large extent on very particular gestures and movements (e.g., to encourage tugging, one must handle the dog and the toy in a particular way, and specific movements are used to improve the dog's grip of the toy), very few written materials were ever published on the specifics of the method, although, as I recollect, it was certainly the most popular topic of discussion on the first dog-related Internet discussion groups in the 1990s.

Turn to Emotional-Cognitive Education (Teaching)

The publication of John Fisher's *Okiem psa* (Think Dog!) in 1994 by PWRil, a prominent local publishing house, can be credited with the popularization of absolutely innovative training methods, increased interest in scientific explanations of dogs' activities, and a new look at the theory of dominance. This first ever textbook on canine psychology available on the Polish market was a huge step toward emotional education and facilitated interspecies communication.[7] As Fisher writes:

> If we were to stand back and examine the dog for what it is, we would realise how silly it is to place human values on the things they do—and examining the dog, for what it really is, is what this book is all about. If we can understand more about dogs, what motivates them, what their values are, how they learn and why they do what they do, then this greater understanding will help us to form a more enjoyable relationship with them. (Fisher, 1991, p. 2)

Knowledge of the laws governing a wolf pack was supposed to help in understanding canine psychology. Fisher also points out that the position of alpha, the leader of the pack, is not obtained and maintained through constant displays of aggression to other members of the pack but that the leader's authority is strengthened by displays of submission and respect from the other members. The alpha wolf is, therefore, somewhat "pushed" into this position, and the wolf pack usually coexists in harmony and cooperates in the fight for survival. Dogs, as Fisher wrote in the early 1990s, are pack animals and have a natural need of being members of a pack and maintaining its hierarchy. When they enter human homes, they treat the family as a substitute pack. Fisher believed that in a multi-species "pack" the human may often unconsciously transfer the responsibilities and rights of the leader onto the dog by pushing him into the alpha position. According to Fisher, the key to peaceful human-canine coexistence is the human entering into the alpha position but not as a result of confrontation and aggression. Fisher writes that it is better to base our relationships with dogs on the rules of a wolf pack and introduce them into everyday life.

The human should thus (1) prevent the dog from using beds, sofas, and armchairs and should sometimes sit on the dog's bedding; alpha sleeps where he wants to sleep and no one can sleep on his bed; (2) before feeding the dog, eat something himself; alpha eats first; (3) control canine play and never let the dog win a play fight; alpha always wins; (4) climb up stairs first and wait for the dog; one shows his respect for alpha by approaching him in submission; (5) pass first through doorways; alpha always goes first; (6) make the dog move if he is in the human's way; when alpha is resting he should not be bothered; and (7) ignore the dog's invitations for play and his solicitations of caresses; it is alpha who always gets what he wants and who signals the hunt (Fisher, 1991, pp. 25–26). Additionally, the guardian should also make sure that the dog earns the right to privileges such as petting, food, and going for a walk by performing some simple task.

This new type of "soft" dominance—devoid of aggression directed at the dog—was enthusiastically welcomed. It should be emphasized that Fisher's theory was based on erroneous precepts and maintained a conformational relationship between human and dog. Despite all these shortcomings, in the 1990s it at least enabled trainers to abandon ritual demonstrations of the human's physical supremacy over the dog. It also introduced simple and easy-to-follow rules governing relations in human-canine packs.

Several years later Fisher became acquainted with the work of, among other scientists, Raymond Coppinger. Fisher revised his views in the short brochure *Understanding the Behaviour of the Pet Dog,* where he admitted that the common practice of implementing dominance programs in the human pack seems to be based on unconfirmed scientific theories (Fisher, 1995). However, this publication was never translated into Polish and the dominance program (the program for lowering a dog's hierarchy in the pack) became firmly entrenched in the minds of many dog guardians and in training protocols. Dominance theory, which has been criticized for many years not only by dog training instructors but also, for more than a decade, by many scientists, behaviorists, and ethologists (cf. Bradshaw, 2011; Coppinger & Coppinger, 2001; Donaldson, 1996; Eaton, 2010; Miklósi, 2009; O'Heare, 2003), not only remains an urban legend but is still present in popular publications on dog training (cf. Millan & Peltier, 2007a, 2007b; Monks of New Skete, 1978).

Criticism of the theory of dominance and the various programs for lowering the dog's position in the pack hierarchy is based on the theory's lack of scientific grounding and focuses on its harmful effects on the human-canine relationship. A confrontational attitude between the human and the canine makes interspecies communication difficult. Creating a set of rules helps the dog to become comfortable in his surroundings. However, these rules should respond to the needs of both sides, in particular the weaker side. A healthy relationship, both between people and between a human and a canine, is based on cooperation, not competition. The myth of the wolf pack exacerbates problems rather than diffusing them. In a way, this myth frees the human from responsibility and from the need to actually teach the animal; it increases the dog's desperation and harms the interspecies bond (cf. Bradshaw, 2011; O'Heare, 2003).

The early 21st century stands witness to the birth of obedience training in Poland based on education, not domination. Many of my students breathed a sigh of relief when I explained to them that the theory of dominance did not help in training but created an aggressive, confrontational relationship between the guardian and the animal. In the opening decade of the new millennium increasingly more Polish trainers, behaviorists, and instructors rejected theories based on competition and promoted techniques based on cooperation and fulfilling the dog's needs.

Fast-Paced Development of Emotional-Cognitive Education (Teaching)

In *Think Dog!* John Fisher not only formulated the concept of "soft" dominance, but he also suggested revolutionary—for the period, the early 1990s—methods of teaching dogs. These methods formed a system which made it possible to elicit desired responses without the use of any kind of force. The method required only "a brain and a piece of food" (Fisher, 1991, p. 45). Almost 10 years before methods using positive reinforcement—based on luring, shaping, and capturing behaviors—became the norm in Poland, Fisher described them in detail, even though he used a different vocabulary than the clicker trainers who came later did.

In his training work with dogs, Fisher abandoned all physical force, justifying his position with so-called negative thigmotaxis, which is an organism's movement away from the source of a negative stimulus. According to Fisher, the response one can expect from a dog being choked to get him to lower his body to the ground, to force him to assume the "down" or "sit" position, is the dog's desire to remain in the standing position—that is, the opposite of the desired response. As a more effective method Fisher proposed to encourage the dog to follow the treat in a way which would make him assume the desired position. Fisher's understanding of what clicker-training expert Karen Pryor referred to as "capturing behaviors" consisted of rewarding the dog when he performed correctly and ignoring him when he did not. Fisher also proposed so-called modeling—that is, the splitting up of entire behaviors into smaller components which lead to the final desired behavior and of rewarding successful completion of each component. Fisher's description of the process of teaching the dog to retrieve is a classic description of the rules of shaping behaviors (Fisher, 1991, pp. 50–51).

As he was incorporating his techniques for working with dogs, Fisher noticed with surprise that methods based in behaviorist psychology are accepted only reluctantly by guardians and are perceived as bribery. Fisher's observations can also be confirmed by the experience of trainers in Poland: When I was switching from "traditional" training methods and making my way toward the exclusive use of positive reinforcement, I often met with guardians who expressed their fears about their dog's potential demoralization and loss of work ethos and that the dog would be working "only to get a hot dog" and not "for the master." The belief that a dog who is being jerked around on a choke collar is working out of love for the guardian coupled with the fear of rewarding the dog for a job well done is something I still find difficult to comprehend.[8]

The founding in 1997 of the *Psy* (Dogs) Internet discussion list, the first Polish online forum for dog lovers,[9] enabled instructors and behaviorists to access specialized publications unavailable in bookstores and became a platform for sharing experiences between people involved in the various aspects of dog fancy as well as a meeting place for Polish speakers living in different geographic locations worldwide. For pet dog guardians, the forum became a treasury of training tips and advice. As stated in a dog-related supplement to the most popular Polish daily newspaper, *Gazeta Wyborcza,* in 2000:

> The website [of the *Psy* Internet discussion list] is the largest Polish-language source of information about dogs on the web. The tips located in the FAQ section will prove the most helpful with raising a dog, solving behavioral problems, teaching the dog various skills. But the website also contains: information about feeding, reviews of "dog books," anecdotes, humor, addresses of dog-friendly accommodations, rulebooks and other helpful information. The discussion list is most probably the liveliest online meeting place of the Polish dog world: experienced trainers, show handlers, veterinarians and regular pet owners. (*Gazeta Wyborcza,* 2000, p. 10)

Members of that dynamic community exchanged experiences and reviewed the information available to them. At the same time, the list became the first venue in Poland for promoting the concept of positive training—that is, training based on positive reinforcement. The main proponent of positive reinforcement was, at the time, Barbara Waldoch, a resident of Australia who was working at the College of Veterinary Medicine at Murdoch University and who had been an active dog trainer for more than 30 years. Waldoch first promoted positive methods on the *Psy* discussion list and then founded the *Kliker* discussion group, which remained an active meeting place for those interested in clicker training for more than 10 years. Because Waldoch spoke fluent English and had access to publications unavailable in Poland, she was a valuable source of information for Polish trainers. She tirelessly shared her training notes and reviewed books and articles, as well as encouraged the translation of valuable training literature into Polish. Interest in her work and the deluge of questions she dealt with encouraged Waldoch to write down her own knowledge and experiences. Finally, in 2002 Waldoch electronically published a book titled *Pozytywne szkolenie psów* (Positive dog training), later published also as a printed book (2007). In her book, Waldoch provides the reader with the theoretical foundations of clicker training and then proceeds to describe in great detail the training techniques for preparing a dog to successfully pass the Polish Companion Dog Exam.[10] Waldoch compared the method she proposed to traditional training this way:

> In contrast to traditional methods, clicker training is based mostly on reinforcement. In this type of training, no behavior is considered incorrect; it may simply not be rewarded at the time (or ever). The dog loses interest in a behavior which is not rewarded and focuses on coming up with a behavior that will make it possible for him to earn a reward. With reinforcement, we can achieve anything we want to achieve, even though this truth may at first seem revolutionary. (Waldoch, 2007, p. 13)

Thanks to Barbara Waldoch and many other members of online communities, as well as the very presence of the Internet, Polish trainers finally had a "window on the world," even if the Polish publishing market remained indifferent to many of the groundbreaking concepts in dog training. Some important books were finally published in Polish, but only after long delays. For example, Jean Donaldson's provocative and inspiring book *The Culture Clash,* first published in the United States in 1996, was published in Poland only in 2007.[11] The book methodically takes apart the theory of dominance, advocates for behaviorist-based training, and shifts the blame for lack of success in training onto the human:

> As soon as you bestow intelligence and morality, you bestow the responsibility that goes along with them.... We set [dogs] up for all kinds of punishment by overestimating their ability to think. Interestingly, it's the so-called "cold" behaviorist model that ends up giving dogs a much better crack at meeting the demands we make of them. The fuzzy-wuzzy model gives dogs problems that they cannot solve and then punishes them for failing. And the saddest thing is that the main association most dogs have with punishment is the presence of their owner.... My argument is that

> dogs aren't demeaned or reduced to the status of laboratory rats by applying what has been learned by behavioral science.... Of all the windows which exist to communicate with dogs, operant conditioning is the window which is open the widest. We should start using it. (Donaldson, 1996, pp. 13–14)

The year 2004 brought about the publication of the Polish translation of Karen Pryor's by then classic (at least in the English-speaking world), *Don't Shoot the Dog.*[12] Pryor's work had been previously known through its recapitulation in Waldoch's book and its summaries on Polish websites. Pryor presents a methodological account of the possibilities of eliminating unwanted behaviors, listing a total of eight methods and describing the advantages of four of them and the disadvantages of the other four (Pryor, 2002, p. 99).

Pryor discusses the consequences of using each method, emphasizing the side effects of using negative methods. Most importantly, she does not use emotionally loaded language, and she does not moralize; what she does is emphasize the effectiveness of positive reinforcement and the scientific—that is, objective—character of the behavioral principles she is presenting:

> Reinforcement training is not a system of reward and punishment—by and large modern trainers don't even use those words. The concept of reward and punishment carries a great freight of emotional associations and interpretations, such as desire and dread and guilt and shoulds and ought to's.... Modern reinforcement training is based not on these folk beliefs but on behavioral science. (Pryor, 2002, p. viii)

Both Waldoch and Pryor are clicker trainers and—at least judging on the basis of the two books discussed here—are representatives of a school of animal training that is indebted to the research on animal behavior carried out first by B. F. Skinner, then by Keller and Marian Breland, and later also by Robert Bailey. Interestingly, the primary goal of the first scientists who influenced the positive training revolution, in particular B. F. Skinner, was not animal welfare but considerations of the effectiveness of training methods. Skinner's preference for positive reinforcement was something of a byproduct. However, the methods were seized by dog trainers not purely because of their effectiveness but largely because the trainers were looking for a way to be kinder to dogs in the process of training. Nevertheless, one of the major objections to clicker training on Polish Internet discussion lists in the late 1990s was its one-size-fits-all approach—that is, the behaviorist assumption that all organisms learn the same way. Dog trainers who had been long used to treating canines as a distinct species opposed clicker training's disregard for the specificity of dogs: for example, the existence of prey drive and distinctions between the predispositions of different breeds (or types) of dogs.

However, the ethological perspective was also changing and began providing tools for humans to communicate with dogs as dogs—tools that went beyond attempts at reproducing the order of the wolf pack. In fact, it was the gradual waning of interest in dogs as descendants of wolves and the growing interest in dogs as a distinct species that proved the most fruitful. Even though Raymond Coppinger's seminal study *Dogs* was never published in Polish, another trainer interested mostly in canine behavior made a large splash. The publication of Norwegian dog trainer Turid Rugaas's book *On Talking Terms With Dogs: Calming Signals*, translated first into English in 1997 and into Polish in 2005, was another groundbreaking moment that reminded contemporary Polish dog trainers of the importance of adding an ethological dimension to their work.[13] Rugaas, a lay authority on dog behavior and communication, points out the existence of a complex, yet subtle, body language that dogs use to avoid conflicts. She presents approximately 30 calming signals and argues that humans can—and should—use them in trying to communicate with dogs. According to Rugaas:

> Dogs … have a language for communication with each other. Canine language in general consists of a large variety of signals using body, face, ears, tail, sounds, movement and expression. The dog's innate ability to signal is easily lost or reinforced through life's experience. If we study the signals dogs use with each other and

use them ourselves, we increase our ability to communicate with our dogs. (Rugaas, 2006, p. 3)

Rugaas's own work on observing and classifying calming signals led her to emphasize the existence of stress in dog training and provided tools for minimizing stress through the acknowledgment and use of calming signals, kindness, and respect for the dog. Not only was Rugaas's book published in Polish relatively quickly, four years before the publication of the translation Rugaas visited Poland for the first time, in March of 2001, to give a seminar on calming signals. This began a series of visits by Rugaas to Poland and a course for instructors. While some of her observations remain controversial—in particular as related to events and activities triggering stress—the existence of calming signals has recently been proved in articles published in peer-reviewed journals (Gazzano et al., 2014). In her seminars Rugaas also consistently uses the analogy of a dog's guardian being like a child's parent.

By the time Rugaas completed her series of visits to Poland, the information available to Polish dog trainers was more or less up-to-date. Polish trainers could read about training based on positive reinforcement and the sensitivity to the dog's emotions that should accompany this type of training; responsibility for the process of training being placed on the trainer; desensitizing and gentle ways of working with difficult dogs; the dog's skills and needs and how to fulfill these needs; and mutual communication. All of this information helped Polish instructors to strengthen the emotional-motivational aspect of their educational activities and to increase their effectiveness on the cognitive-intellectual level. This is not to say that traditional training, based on the contrast method, has completely disappeared, but most certainly the trend is toward positive training.

Subsequent years have not brought about any revolutionary ideas, although increased interest in the perspective of cognitive ethology (as opposed to the behaviorist approach) is noticeable—for example, in the recent translations of works by John Bradshaw (Polish translation published in 2012)[14] and Alexandra Horowitz (Polish translation published in 2010).[15] Increasingly more books on dog training are being published, and delays in the publication of translations are growing shorter. Foreign experts often visit Poland and give seminars to an ever growing group of enthusiasts. Globalization, technology (access to the Internet), and Poles' increased knowledge of foreign languages (particularly English) have all played a part in these changes. Finally, one should also mention the explosion of interest in canine performance sports in the 21st century. Here, I am thinking of agility, dummy trials, sheepdog trials, dogtrekking, disc trials, and the like. This explosion is discussed in this volume by Justyna Włodarczyk in Chapter 3. Elsewhere, Włodarczyk also explores the gendered aspects of canine performance sports on the example of canine agility in Poland (Włodarczyk, 2016). All these changes prove the strengthening of the tendency toward emotional-motivational activities, which, in my eyes, bodes well for the further development of the human-canine bond in Poland.

Notes

1. Cynagogy: a neologism created by the author from the Greek *kynagogos* (literally, "leading the dog"), analogous to the word *pedagogy.*
2. Coppinger assumes that dogs were not created through artificial selection, that is, through purposeful human activity (as Darwin had assumed), but that their appearance was the result of natural selection: domestication (genetic), tameness (genetic), and trainability (Coppinger & Coppinger, 2001, p. 57).
3. As Coppinger claims, the mortality of wolf pups in natural conditions is 70 percent to 90 percent (Coppinger & Coppinger, 2001, p. 59).
4. Flight distance represents how close an animal will allow humans to get before it runs away.
5. These books have been translated into Polish and published in the 21st century: Millan, C., & Peltier, M. J. (2011). *Zaklinacz psów. Proste metody rozwiązywania problemów twojego psa* [Cesar's way: The natural, everyday guide to understanding and correcting common dog problems] (R. Palusiński, Trans.). Warsaw, Poland: Illuminatio; Millan, C., & Peltier, M. J. (2012). *Jak zostać przywódcą stada* [Be the pack leader] (M. Lorenc, Trans.). Warsaw, Poland: Illuminatio; Mnisi z New Skete [Monks of New Skete].(2004). *Jak być najlepszym przyjacielem psa* (M. Redlicki& A. Redlicka, Trans.). Łódź, Poland: Galaktyka.

6. This does not mean that all trainers abandoned the use of aversive stimuli, nor that the tools of the trade disappeared from the market.
7. Fisher, J. (1994). *Okiem psa* (M. Caprari, trans.) Warsaw, Poland: PWRiL.
8. When I was still using "the contrast method," I rarely had to remind the handlers to issue a correction, while my cue to reward the dogs needed to be repeated many times. Praising and recognizing good work is something people often seem to find unnecessary in dog training, while they somehow feel obliged to correct any mistakes.
9. The list was created by the author and Grzegorz Mucha and was accompanied by a website.
10. The official Polish dog obedience examination, administered by the Polish Kennel Club.
11. Book published in Poland as: Donaldson, J. (2007). *Pies i człowiek. Jak żyć zgodnie pod jednym dachem* (M. Redlicki, Trans.). Łódź, Poland: Galaktyka.
12. Book published in Poland as: Pryor, K. (2004). *Najpierw wytresuj kurczaka* (B. Ludwiczak, Trans.). Poznań, Poland: Media Rodzina.
13. Book published in Poland as: Rugaas, T. (2005). *Sygnały uspokajające. Jak psy unikają konfliktów* (M. Grossman-Klieber, Trans.). Łódź, Poland: Galaktyka.
14. Bradshaw, J. (2012). *Zrozumieć psa. Jak być jego lepszym przyjacielem* (E. Abłamowicz, Trans.). Warsaw, Poland: Czarna Owca.
15. Horowitz, A. (2010). *Oczami psa. Co psy widzą, czują i wiedzą* (M. Bugajska, Trans.). Warsaw, Poland: Czarna Owca.

References

Bradshaw, J. (2011). *Dog sense: How the new science of dog behavior can make you a better friend to your pet.* New York, NY: Basic Books.

Brzezicha, A. (1997). *Mój pies—amatorskie szkolenie* [My dog: Amateur training]. Warsaw, Poland: Mada.

Brzezicha, A. (2002). *Twój pies. Podstawy wychowania i szkolenia* [Your dog: The basics of upbringing and training]. Warsaw, Poland: Mada.

Coppinger, R., & Coppinger, L. (2001). *Dogs. A new understanding of canine origin, behavior, and evolution.* Chicago, IL: University of Chicago Press.

Donaldson, J. (1996). *The culture clash.* Berkeley, CA: James & Kenneth Publishers.

Eaton, B. (2010). *Dominance in dogs: Fact or fiction?* Wenatchee, WA: Dogwise Publishing.

Fisher, J. (1991). *Think dog! An owner's guide to canine psychology.* North Pomfret, VT: Trafalgar Square Publishing.

Fisher, J. (1995). *Understanding the behaviour of the pet dog: A discussion paper on dominance and other matters.* Tisbury, UK: COAPE.

Gazeta Wyborcza. (2000, June 10). Hau, hau w Internecie [Bow-wow on the Internet]. Hau Hau No. 0, a supplement to *Gazeta Wyborcza, 234,* 10.

Gazzano, A., Zilocchi, M., Ricci, E., Falaschi, C., Bedini, M., Guardini, G., & Mariti, C. (2014). Calming signals in dogs: From myth to scientific reality? *Veterinaria (Cremona), 28*(1), 15–20.

Gieżyński, J. (1958). *Amatorska tresura psów użytkowo-obronnych* [Amateur training of protection-utility dogs]. Warsaw, Poland: PWRiL.

Gieżyński, J. (1964). *Szkolenie psów myśliwskich* [Training hunting dogs]. Warsaw, Poland: PWRiL.

Knowles, M. S. (1968). Andragogy, not pedagogy. *Adult Leadership, 16*(10), 350–352.

Merriam, S. B. (2001). Andragogy and self-directed learning: Pillars of adult learning theory. *New Directions for Adult and Continuing Education, 89,* 3–14. http://dx.doi.org/10.1002/ace.3

Miklósi, A. (2009). *Dog behaviour, evolution* and *cognition.* Oxford, UK: Oxford University Press.

Millan, C., & Peltier, M. J. (2007a). *Cesar's way: The natural, everyday guide to understanding and correcting common dog problems.* New York, NY: Three Rivers Press.

Millan, C., & Peltier, M. J. (2007b). *Be the pack leader: Use Cesar's way to transform your dog … and your life.* New York, NY: Three Rivers Press.

Monks of New Skete (1978). *How to be your dog's best friend.* New York, NY: Little, Brown and Company.

Most, K. (2000). *Training dogs: A manual.* Wenatchee, WA: Dogwise Publishing. (Original work published 1910; reprint of 1954 translation, J. Cleugh, trans.)

Niemierko, B. (2007). *Kształcenie szkolne. Podręcznik skutecznej dydaktyki* [School education: The handbook of effective teaching]. Warsaw, Poland: Wydawnictwa Akademickie I Profesjonalne.

O'Heare, J. (2003). *Dominance theory and dogs.* Ottawa, Canada: DogPsych.

Pryor, K. (2002). *Don't shoot the dog: The new art of teaching and training*. Lydney, UK: Ringpress Books.

Rugaas, T. (2006). *On talking terms with dogs: Calming signals* (2nd ed.). Wenatchee, WA: Dogwise Publishing.

Skinner, B. F. (1938). *The behavior of organisms*. New York, NY: Appleton-Century-Crofts.

Smyczyński, L. (1989). *Psy, rasy, hodowla, szkolenie* [Dogs, breeds, breeding, training]. Katowice, Poland: Uniwersum. (Original work published 1948)

Waldoch, B. (2007). *Pozytywne szkolenie psów* [Positive dog training]. Lublin, Poland: Werset.

Włodarczyk, J. (2016). Post-communist canine: A feminist approach to women and dogs in canine performance sports in Poland. *Society & Animals, 24*(2), 129–152.

3

Canine Performance Sports in Poland: Another Look at the Dog Training Revolution

Justyna Włodarczyk

Watching performances of Poland's top competitive obedience teams at the 2015 qualifications for the *Fédération Cynologique Internationale* (FCI) World Championships, it is easy to observe the dogs' joy when performing the exercises.[1] Their tails are almost constantly wagging; their gaze is fixed on their handlers' faces; their responses to the commands are brisk and enthusiastically joyful. The dogs seem to be excited in anticipation of the tasks awaiting them; yet, it is an enthusiasm which is under control, curbed—at least as it appears—by the dogs' own internal motivation, not by leashes or collars. In contrast, the behavior of dogs in an instructional obedience video dated 1991, scripted and directed by communist Poland's most well-known dog trainer, Antoni Brzezicha, is strikingly different: As the dogs go through their paces, their heads and tails are invariably down, their movements cautious and slow (Brzezicha, 1991).[2] The dogs seem to be performing without much joy, grudgingly complying with the handlers' demands. They invariably lag behind their handlers in off-leash exercises and rarely maintain eye contact with their humans, often displaying other signs of discomfort and stress, such as licking and sniffing the ground—signs evident to the eye of a spectator with even a rudimentary knowledge of canine ethology. The change is glaring and—from the contemporary point of view—it is difficult not to ask: Did the handlers and judges not see that the dogs were not enjoying themselves? Why did the judges not demand (and reward) a more joyful performance? Why were the trainers unable to elicit such a performance?

These are all questions asked from a 21st-century perspective and they are valid only within a contemporary mindset: one in which the goal of training is defined differently than it had been 25 years ago. Clearly, what must have happened in the meantime, between 1991 and 2015, is not simply a change of training methods but a change of training philosophy. In 1991 the judge saw nothing wrong with the performances he observed. On the contrary, the dogs were rewarded precisely because their behavior reflected the prevailing understanding of the human-canine relationship at the time: the dog was expected to submit to the human. There is little joy in forced submission; thus, joy would not have been an expected element of the dog's performance. The performances from the 2015 top-level obedience competitors suggest that value is now placed on the dog's enjoyment of the process of training and, simultaneously, also on the strength and beauty of the resulting human-canine bond.

The purpose of this chapter is to theorize the changes in dog training philosophy geared toward competitive canine events based on training materials (instructional articles, videos, rule books, and interviews published in popular media) available in Poland from the 1970s to the present. The goal is to show not only how training methods have changed but also how expectations related to the dog's performance have changed along with them. Such an interpretation reveals how changes in training are part of a broader redefinition of the human-canine bond and reflect changes in the dog's place in contemporary Polish society. In this chapter I argue that the emergence of a plethora of new canine performance events in the early 21st century is itself entangled in these changes. It is a sign that dog guardians are actively seeking new ways of interacting with their dogs: ways that reflect postmodern notions of identity, exhibit a changed understanding of what it means to care for a dog, and prioritize the nurturing of canine happiness over expectations of blind submission.

Background: Theorizing the Training Revolution

Even though throughout the period under analysis there coexisted a variety of training methods, a shift toward what is broadly dubbed as positive methods is clearly visible in Poland, as described by Agnieszka Orłowska in Chapter 2. The term *positive methods* is in itself a very imprecise umbrella term; yet, most trainers who use positive methods underscore their preference for what is defined in Skinnerian behaviorism as positive reinforcement. While Skinner's training protocols were designed with emphasis on greater effectiveness of the training process and his aversion to punishment was based on the empirical observation of the side effects of applying aversive stimuli (Skinner, 1938, 1971/1976), many companion animal trainers in the English-speaking world (the most popular names include Ian Dunbar, Karen Pryor, Jean Donaldson, Pamela Dennison, and Patricia McConnell) embraced these techniques from the 1980s onward, not solely because of their effectiveness but primarily because of their humane character (Pręgowski, 2015). In *The Companion Species Manifesto,* Donna Haraway famously refers to the rush to embrace the new training methods using emotionally charged vocabulary as "near-religious conversion from the military-style Koehler dog training methods, not so fondly remembered for corrections like leash jerks and ear pinches to the joys of rapidly delivering liver cookies" (Haraway, 2003, p. 48). For Haraway, training is a process of "becoming with" (Haraway, 2007, pp. 95–132), a definition that emphasizes the role of intersubjective empathy. Empathy for the dog's experience and respect for the dog as a nonhuman other are key concepts in the narrative of the training revolution from the perspective of animal welfare. This shift toward "kinder, gentler" methods is commonly read as being embedded in the growing aversion to the use of physical force in interpersonal relationships, visible, also, for example, in childrearing and schooling (Koski & Bäcklund, 2015) and in the increased value of empathy in contemporary Western societies.

Using the language of ethology, the training revolution is interpreted as a move away from the so-called dominance model—that is, a crude, and incorrect, transference of the wolf pack theory onto human-canine relations (cf. Coppinger & Coppinger, 2001; Eaton, 2008; Miklósi, 2009).

The ethological analysis of changes in training methods stresses developments in scientific knowledge of canine behavior and human-canine interaction and their resulting incorporation into animal training protocols. The work of Norwegian trainer Turid Rugaas, discussed in Chapter 2, also falls into this category: It is because of her close observation of canine behavior that Rugaas develops new methods of training that do not result in the dog's discomfort.

While these two perspectives are most certainly important, they are not exhaustive. The shift in training methods can also be analyzed using a different vocabulary, that of critical cultural theory. For example, the switch from force to kindness can be most broadly defined using Foucault's modalities of power as a shift from sovereign power to disciplinary power, but even more specifically as a move—within the disciplinary mode—away from reliance on the panoptical model (where it is the possibility of being watched which guarantees compliance with the rules) to an active desire for performing correctly regardless of the presence of a supervisor. The resulting human-canine training relationship in positive training has also been described using Foucault's definition of pastoral power (Włodarczyk, 2014). In Cary Wolfe's *Zoontologies,* Paul Patton, writing about horses, recognizes the power dynamic inherent in the training relationship and uses a Foucauldian vocabulary to identify the various technologies of exercising power, arguing that even the most sympathetic training techniques are coercive in that they cause the animal to behave in ways in which it otherwise would not (Patton, 2003). Patton's interpretation of training can be read as leading to the conclusion that positive training is positive only from the perspective of Skinner's quadrant. However, this does not mean for Patton that training should be abandoned wholesale. Conscious of Foucault's complex understanding of power, Patton suggests that animal training makes us aware that ethical relations are possible not only between equals. Patton does, however, suggest that the aesthetico-moral defense of animal training is corrupt because training—no matter how positive—is still embedded in the human value system and the entire effort of training an animal is a process of making the animal share the human's values: what changes is the sophistication of the methods (Patton, 2003, p. 93).

Competitive Dog Training Events Before 1989

While this chapter focuses on the significance of the current explosion of activities on the canine sports scene, a few words are due on dog training events in Poland before 1989, with emphasis on the types of activities available and the definition of the human-canine bond in the rule books of these events. Dog training competitions in Poland between World War II and 1989, with the exception of conformation shows, were relatively few and far between. The events that did take place can be divided into three major groups: obedience competitions and exams, protection dog competitions and exams, and various types of hunting dog competitions and exams. With the exception of obedience competitions, the events were closely tied to dogs' presumed usefulness to humans, and even obedience exercises were presented as a more publicly available version of exercises for working dogs (meaning: police dogs and military dogs).

The first field trials in communist Poland, organized according to British rules, took place in 1959. Trials organized according to Polish rules and targeted at a larger group of hunting breeds were organized shortly afterward, in 1962 (Bukład, 2010, p. 3). The *Regulamin prób i konkursów pracy psów myśliwskich* (Regulations of Field Trials and Tests for Hunting Dogs) stated—and still state—the purpose of the events as "popularizing hunting with dogs through the testing and constant improvement of the usefulness of hunting dogs" (Związek Kynologiczny w Polsce, 2007, p. 2). According to Ewa Bukład, the first obedience event, a so-called obedience ring, took place at the National Dog Show in Cracow in 1959. The first official obedience trial—organized in a format differing from contemporary competitive obedience and called a companion dog examination—took place in 1960 and was attended by four dogs: three German Shepherds and one Boxer, handled by three men and one woman. Interestingly, the rules of the obedience examinations were based on the rules of the American Kennel Club. Just like in the United States, the dogs were able to obtain the titles of Companion Dog, Companion Dog Excellent, and Utility Dog. The first official, thorough, and comprehensive rule book for the *Regulamin szkolenia, egzaminów i zawodów psa towarzyszącego i psa obrończego* (Companion Dog and Protection Dog Exams and Trials), prepared by Antoni Brzezicha, was published only in 1979 and was 115 pages long. The words *utility* and *usefulness* appear practically on every other page of the booklet, while the main goal of obedience training exams is listed as "verifying the degree to which the dog submits to the handler," with the main goal of dog training defined as "establishing the utility and breeding quality of dogs" (Związek Kynologiczny w Polsce, 1979). There is no mention of improving the emotional bond between the human and the dog.

In the 1970s the significance of *Pies Obronny* (Protection Dog) exams grew, and training began to be associated with teaching dogs when and how to attack potential muggers and other assailants. This was due largely to the influence of retired police and military personnel (Władysław Chyrc, Antoni Brzezicha, Andrzej Woźniakowski), who practically monopolized training courses and also authored most of the training manuals. Protection Dog exams were divided into three components: obedience, protection, and tracking. This meant that Protection Dog exams and competitions had a much higher status than Companion Dog competitions because they contained within themselves obedience as a component. Many dogs trialed in both protection championships and obedience championships. The *Mistrzostwa Polski Psów Obrończych* (National Protection Dog Championships) were organized in 1972 and the *Mistrzostwa Polski Psów Towarzyszących* (National Companion Dog Championships) in 1980 (Brzezicha, 1980, p. 14). In 1979, 44 dogs took part in the National Protection Dogs Championships (Brzezicha, 1980, p. 14), while in 2013 the same championship event attracted only 32 participants. Interest in protection dog sports has significantly decreased since 1989.

Competitive Dog Training Events After 1989

Training events in communist Poland were explicitly geared toward proving dogs' usefulness to humans. Meanwhile, contemporary canine performance events seem to reverse this logic and try to prove humans' usefulness to dogs—that is, they are attempts at finding activities that function as substitute outlets for a bored urban dog's energy. They function more as entertainment for the dog and a bonding activity for the canine and the human. The outburst of interest in different kinds of canine performance sports in the late 1990s and in the 2000s in Poland and other Eastern European countries poses a challenge to Paul Patton's claim that

> the aesthetico-moral defense of the activities for which animals are trained is corrupt in the same manner to the extent that it misrepresents what, anthropomorphically, we might call the "values" of the animals involved and it projects onto them as natural certain aptitudes and airs that are valued by their all too human trainers. (Patton, 2003, p. 93)

While Patton claims that top-level competitive training is about sophisticated techniques of making the animal share the goals of the trainer (the later work by Foucault on the ethics of self-care can come in handy here to describe how this is achieved and can offer an alternative framework to the master-slave metaphor), the explosion of canine-related competitive (and semi-competitive) events in the 2000s counters this claim, at least explicitly, because these new activities are designed as outlets for a dog's "natural" needs, albeit in a new, modern, and urban context.

It seems that instead of instilling the values of the human in the dog, the existence of this trend suggests that the "values" of the dog now determine the activity the human and dog engage in. The human chooses from a plethora of activities available, basing her (less often: his) choice on the dog's talents and aptitudes—on the dog's desires. In other words, I pose that the very existence of the canine events scene is a reflection of the changes in the human-canine relationship. Dog training ceases to be what postmodern thinkers refer to as a "grand narrative"—that is, a universalizing explanation and legitimation of existing power relations (Lyotard, 1984). In other words, it ceases to be about naturalizing human domination over animals. This big narrative breaks up in little narratives *(petits recits)*, in which the guardian follows the dog's individual aptitudes and talents even if they lead in unexpected directions. This is not to say that training relationships in the new performance sports are not power relationships. Of course they are, but they also take into account dog agency and, interestingly, their arrival corresponds in time with the outburst in positive training methods. Most of the new sports explicitly endorse positive training techniques in the rule books.

Concurrently, a survey of the motivation of Polish participants in canine-related sports activities carried out in the period 2010–2011 on a group of 150 participants proved that the humans' motivation for participating in such activities is their desire to deepen the emotional bond with their dogs, to find an outlet for the dog's energy, and to make new friends and be a part of a social group (Teodorowicz & Woźniewicz-Dobrzyńska, 2014). As an aside, the research also revealed that the respondents were predominantly female (65 percent), urban dwellers, and significantly younger than suggested by results of similar research carried out in other countries, for example Canada (Farrell, Hope, Hulstein, & Spaulding, 2015). In fact, when respondents were asked about whether any humans accompany them at dog training events, many pointed to their parents, and the age of the respondents ranged from 11 to 50 years (Teodorowicz & Woźniewicz-Dobrzyńska, 2014, p. 302). These findings are in stark contrast to those of Farell et al. (2015) and Hultsman (2012) and reveal the Polish dog sports participants to be much younger than their counterparts in the United States and Canada. Research from Finland, carried out on a group of participants in competitive obedience, revealed the group to be 100 percent female and also younger than the North American dog sports enthusiasts (Koski & Bäcklund, 2015). Although some of the Polish respondents were even younger than the Finnish ones, it should be mentioned that the Polish survey was distributed via Internet channels, and some older respondents may have been reluctant to participate in this form of research. The respondents were also aware of their dog's aptitude (or lack thereof) for a particular sport and selected the activity on the basis of their dog's talents (Teodorowicz & Woźniewicz-Dobrzyńska, 2014, p. 301). It should be noted that by 2010 already many forms of recreation and sport were available for interested dog guardians.

A brief look at the history of canine performance events in Poland reveals that in the mid-2000s these quickly began multiplying in numbers. At the time of writing in 2015, the canine events scene in Poland consists of multiple sports that appeared only after the systemic transformation of 1989:

- Obedience (FCI rules)
- Rally obedience
- Agility
- Canine disc (also known as dogfrisbee)
- Mantrailing
- Flyball (two reams of dogs race across a set of hurdles to retrieve a tennis ball)
- Dummy trials (a derivative of field trials but the dog retrieves a plastic dummy, not a real bird)
- Search and rescue (while not a competitive event, this activity only opened up to amateurs after 1989 and involves a multiple-level certification program)
- Weight-pulling
- Water rescue (similarly to search and rescue, the certification program is open to all dogs)
- Dogtrekking
- Herding trials
- Various kinds of mushing events (including canicross)
- Bikejoring (dog runs alongside a bicycle)
- Dock diving (dogs jumping into a pool off a dock, longest jump wins)
- Speedway (basically a timed recall to handler contest)
- Canine freestyle (also known as doggy dancing)
- Treibball (the "herding" of inflatable plastic balls)

The classic trio of canine sports practiced in communist Poland—obedience (by local Polish rules), protection trials, and hunting trials—have been pushed to the margins of the canine sports scene, although they are still present. Men still dominate protection and field trials (Włodarczyk, 2014).

One of the new performance sports is dock diving. Dogs are asked to leap into a special pool, and the longest jump wins. This competition has significant spectator appeal. (Copyright by K9Action [Tomasz Mońko], www.k9action.eu. Courtesy of Tomasz Mońko.)

Agility is the oldest among the new arrivals: the first sanctioned agility trials were organized in the early 1990s. However, the number of trials increased only in the mid-2000s, with the largest events gathering up to 400 participants from several neighboring countries (Włodarczyk, 2014). The Polish team regularly participates in FCI Agility World Championships, and in recent years the members have been quite successful on the international arena. The first Polish competitor to win a medal at the World Championships was Olga Kwiecień with her Pyrenean Shepherd Brava, in 2012. While the agility regulations do not explicitly encourage the use of positive methods, they do emphasize that agility "is an educational and sporting activity intended to improve the dog's integration into society. The sport requires a good rapport between dog and handler, which will result in perfect understanding" (Fédération Cynologique Internationale, 2012a). "Integration into society" is, of course, something of a blanket term, but it does underscore that which I have been emphasizing as the general impulse of modern canine performance events: the inclusion of the dog as "a significant other" (using Haraway's term from *The Companion Species Manifesto*) in the human's everyday life practices. In Poland, and not only there (Farell et al., 2015; Hultsman, 2012), agility is a sport dominated by women and practiced largely by city dwellers.

Agility is usually taught through increasingly sophisticated techniques that build on the dog's prey drive. While not all training may be "purely positive" (from the perspective of Skinner's quadrant, and from other perspectives as well), all handbooks emphasize the "fun" aspect of the sport and its role as a remedy for canine boredom. It is not coincidental that the title of the first agility handbook published in Polish is *Agility. Sport i zabawa* (Agility: Sport and fun).[3] Similarly, it is not coincidental that the book's reviews emphasize that one of its advantages is in displaying that agility is something new on the dog training scene because "the entire process is fun; it serves the purpose of alleviating boredom and strengthening the bond one has with one's pet. This is not strict obedience training, where a scared dog submits to the owner" (Café Animal, 2010).

Canine disc is one of the activities in which Polish competitors shine on the international arena, a result of the determination of one individual who almost single-handedly devoted his life to promoting the sport among Polish dog guardians. Dariusz Radomski organized the first canine disc event in Poland in 2005, and already in 2012 Poland hosted the European Championships, where over 300 players from all over the world (including Japan) participated in the three-day event in a beautiful urban park. As of 2015, local Polish trials bring together approximately 200 human-canine teams and are quite impressive in scope, often generating the interest of local and national media and attracting crowds of spectators. Similarly to agility, though in an even more obvious way, canine disc is also based on a redirection of the dog's prey drive (the desire to chase and intercept fleeing prey) transferred onto an inanimate object: a plastic disc. Radomski advertises the sport as a possible lifesaver for the unruly and disobedient dog—the dog whose owner cannot keep him from chasing cars and bicycles or destroying furniture. In an interview with *Dog&Sport,* a quarterly magazine published in Polish and devoted solely to canine performance sports (and with a circulation of

17,000!), Radomski writes that "a serious advantage of dogfrisbee is its availability.... All you need is discs and a field in a park or your backyard" (Radomski, 2010, p. 5). While it remains to be examined whether the top dogs in the sport are truly obedience school dropouts who have found a sense of purpose in catching plastic, the sport does attract a crowd of participants who see it as a fun outlet for a dog's excessive energy and for whom the competitive aspect of the activity is secondary. Paula Gumińska, one of Poland's top players, claims that her dog, Wena, "takes part in trials but for her it is all fun, it's like catching prey.... There are no commands, no coercion. For her, it's just the pleasure of catching a disc" (Stenzel, 2012).

Both agility and canine disc are sports that function as substitute outlets for a dog's prey drive. Consequently, it is the dogs whose prey drive is the most developed who have a competitive advantage over others in these sports (although other factors cannot be discounted), but a number of competitive events not explicitly based on prey drive have appeared. One of them is dogtrekking: a cross between orienteering and taking the dog out for a walk. Here, human-canine teams, with map and compass in hand, tackle a course designed specifically to highlight the beauty of the landscape. This is a timed event, and the team with the shortest time (and that hits all checkpoints along the route) wins. Canicross is a faster paced version of this endeavor: there are no check points and the route is well marked, with the stroll turning into a long-distance race.

Since 2003, when the first event was organized in Poland, dogtrekking has exploded in popularity, becoming one of the favorite events for parents with children (Bonk, 2010, p. 4). The "Family" category is developing the most rapidly, while entries in all categories average approximately 200 teams per event. Dogtrekking does not require sophisticated training techniques, though it certainly helps if the dog is willing to pull the handler and is not easily distracted by the presence other dogs. It does not even require a recall, as the dogs are always on leash (as stipulated by the regulations). The team's success depends mostly on the handler's stamina and orienteering skills, but for most participants the competitive aspect is absolutely secondary. The sport is a way of including the dog in an individual human's (sometimes family's) passion for hiking in the outdoors, while providing the dog with much-needed exercise. The discipline's selling point is, in fact, its laid-back and noncompetitive character (Bonk, 2010, pp. 5–6).

Mantrailing, which is basically tracking the scent of a human being, is also a semi-competitive event whose popularity is growing among canine guardians. While the obedience and protection dog exams in communist Poland often included a tracking component, the dog's performance on the track was judged according to very strict criteria: the dog's head had to be down, he had to be moving at a steady pace, and he had to indicate each turn of the track in a precise way, as specified in the *Regulamin szkolenia, egzaminów i zawodów psa towarzyszącego i psa obrończego* (Regulations of Training, Exams and Competitions for Companion Dogs and Protection Dogs; Związek Kynologiczny w Polsce, 1979). Points were lost each time the dog went off track or raised his head. In contrast, mantrailing tracks are evaluated on a pass or fail basis: the dog has to find the person hidden at the end of the track. It is telling that the rules of Mantrailing Competency Tests (known in Polish as SKOP, or *Sprawdzian Kompetencji Zespołów Tropienia Użytkowego*) describe the activity not as proving the dog's usefulness to humans (as had been the case with tracking tests under communism) but as "a form of activity that naturally creates a strong human-canine bond and leads to mutual respect and trust" (SKOP, 2014).

This outburst of variety in canine-related activities can be interpreted with regard to the notion of individualization, which has been employed by various theorists (cf. Beck, 1992; Beck & Beck-Gernsheim, 2002; Giddens, 1991, 1994) to explain how postmodern individuals are faced with an increased number of choices they must make to shape their life in a way that best reflects their perceived individuality. Ulrich Beck also argues that individualization is connected to changes in social and family structure: the individual has replaced social class or the nuclear family as the fundamental unit of social reproduction (Beck & Beck-Gernsheim, 2002). However, the dog is no mere accessory to the human individual; bearing in mind how concerned the guardians are with choosing the "right" activity for their dog, one can rather speak of extending the notion of individualization onto the canine partner. Of course it is the human who makes the choice, but this choice is then evaluated through establishing the dog's level of enjoyment of the activity. It is not uncommon on the Polish dog sports scene to switch between sports should a dog not exhibit enjoyment, or to try several activities with a young dog and continue with the one which the dog finds the most "fun." Farrell et al.'s (2015) research performed in Canada suggests this is also the case there, and while the research conducted in Poland did not focus on motivations for changing the activities the human-canine team is involved in, I (with knowledge of the dog sports scene resulting from long years of personal involvement) know of numerous such cases. These include an individual who acquired a dog with the specific purpose of participating in flyball and finally ended up participating (quite intensively and with great success) in mantrailing because the dog did not "enjoy" the sport of flyball. In other words, the humans are often willing to significantly alter their life plans, switch between different social groups, and adopt different value systems, all because they see it as being in the best interest of their dog.

The emergence of the canine sports scene is also a reflection of Poland's transition into a free market economy: the human consumers choose—from a variety of options—the product that they see as the best suited to the needs of the human-canine team they represent. While the talents and aptitude of the dog are listed as primary decisive factors, the human's preferences are certainly also taken into account. Nature lovers can choose dogtrekking; those who enjoy being in the spotlight will love the applause of awed crowds at canine disc events; while flyball fans claim that nothing can beat the sense of teamwork and human camaraderie generated in that sport. In turn, each sport entices would-be aficionados with promises of a uniquely crafted "fun" experience. In fact, the sports seem to be vying for the title of the "most positive" sport: the one which promises to deliver the most enjoyable experience. The strategy assumed by many of the sports consists of breaking the association between that particular sport and the traditional understanding of dog obedience.

Competitive Obedience: Redefining Fun

Competitive obedience is a particularly interesting case among competitive dog sports because it is one of the few activities that predate the current outburst of canine performance sports. Obedience trials did take place before 1989, but their purpose was defined differently than it is now. Until the first years of the 21st century the scoring of competitive obedience events, organized according to local rules of the Polish Kennel Club, reflected the dominant take on the human-canine relationship. As the voice-over in Antoni Brzezicha's video explained, the purpose of obedience competitions was to demonstrate the dog's usefulness to humans and the human's skill at subduing the animal (Brzezicha, 1991). In the judging of the exercises emphasis was placed on precision of the dog's performance, not on speed or the dog's apparent enjoyment of the exercises.

Many of the competitive events that have appeared in the 21st century define themselves in stark opposition to the old understanding of dog obedience, as evident from the excerpts from various rule books quoted earlier. In post-communist Poland, in light of the outburst of canine-related sports and recreational activities and the concurrent redefinition of the human-canine bond, the sport of obedience found itself with something of a public relations problem. Modern dog guardians no longer wished to participate in an activity that defined itself as testing the human's skills at forcing the dog to submit. What has helped the sport is a much-needed makeover, initiated by the adoption of new, international rules.

While competitive exams and trials testing a dog's knowledge of training exercises did exist in communist Poland, the FCI-sanctioned sport of dog obedience entered Poland only in the 21st century (first official trial: April 2004 in Błażejewko). To break the connection with the military drill associated with traditional training, even the name of the sport was changed from the Polish *posłuszeństwo* to the English "obedience" (never translated into Polish in the new FCI rules). This move speaks to Poles' fascination with "everything Western" and is in line with the naming of all of the new events, which are also referred to using English. While the actual exercises of the old-style Polish obedience did not differ significantly from the new FCI obedience exercises, the new sport was marketed as requiring the use of positive training methods. Maria Kuncewicz, sometimes referred to as the godmother of obedience in Poland because she was the *spiritus movens* behind the effort to translate the regulations and organize the first trials (at which she served as a steward), advertised the new sport this way in 2004:

> Obedience is gaining new fans because it emphasizes the contact and communication between handler and dog. There is no place here for "breaking" a dog, showing him who the boss is. Teamwork has to be pleasant both for the dog and for the handler. As such, this sport comes to us at a timely moment when we are beginning to treat dogs not as blindly submissive animals carrying out our orders, but are starting to focus on developing their willingness to COOPERATE with us.[4]

Competitive obedience is a sport in which handler and dog perform a series of exercises, such as heeling, retrieving, send-aways, and are judged according to how closely their execution conforms to the written description of the exercise in the rule book. In the FCI version of the sport—that is, according to the rules which govern how the exercises are judged in the majority of European countries—additional points are given for a team's "general impression." Additionally, per the current FCI regulations, during the performance of each exercise a dog must exhibit willingness and brisk speed. To quote the regulations: "When judging the general impression, the dog's willingness to work and obey the commands is essential.... To get a high score both handler and dog must ... show mutual enjoyment" (Fédération Cynologique Internationale, 2012b). In other words, a dog's overall demeanor, the appearance of canine happiness, is rewarded with a better score. Dogs which seem to be bursting with enthusiasm and yet are able to curb that enthusiasm score higher than dogs who either lack enthusiasm or are visibly unable to control their emotions (for example, constant barking or jumping are cause for disqualification).

While it is difficult to establish whether the new rules encouraged new methods of training or whether they actually reflected changes that had already been ongoing, it is a fact that most of the top competitors declare, in both printed materials and online training courses, which have become very popular in the past several years, the use of positive methods and their focus on the dog's enjoyment of the training process. In the "Methodology" section of her online obedience courses, Joanna Hewelt, the competitor whose performance was referenced in the opening paragraph of this chapter and who is also a very popular obedience instructor, writes: "Our priority in training is joy, passion and commitment, which consequently leads to a cooperating team: a smiling human and a smiling dog" (Hewelt, 2013). The trainer's emphasis is not only on the use of treats and other rewards to classically condition training as a pleasant experience but on opening up channels of communication, on creating a stronger bond between the human and the dog. In another article Hewelt writes: "For me, preparing a dog for obedience [competition] is something of a philosophy. I don't want my dogs to see me as a vending machine that might just distribute a hotdog or a ball. I want them to 'talk' to me; to ask me 'what signal will be next'?" (Hewelt, 2014, p. 22). The word *submission* is not in Hewelt's vocabulary, and her attitude is representative of the change that took place between the 1980s and the early 21st century: training should now be fun and its explicit goal to improve human-canine communication.

Despite its makeover, the popularity of obedience still lags behind some of the other canine events, with the biggest trials generating entries usually not exceeding 100 human-canine teams. For example, there were 87 teams entered the first competition in 2013, which took place in the city of Kalisz, and 87 percent of the human competitors were women. Entries in Polish agility and canine disc competitions can exceed these numbers severalfold. Somewhat curiously—though in accordance with the logic governing the proliferation of dog sports—a new obedience-like sport has appeared and promises to be "more fun" than obedience. Rally obedience made its debut on the Polish canine sports scene in 2011. The sport is sanctioned by the Rally-O Association, which explicitly bases its rules on those of the American Association of Professional Dog Trainers. The Polish regulations state the goal of the sport as "developing a positive relationship between the handler and the dog, based on trust and mutual respect" (Rally-O Association, 2015). As an article published in the most popular dog-related magazine in Poland, *Mój Pies* (My dog) claims, rally obedience is even more conducive to the use of positive training methods than classic obedience because "the rigorous rules of obedience restrict communication between the dog and the handler and make cooperation more difficult" (Urban, 2012, p. 22). Rally promises to make the experience of deepening the human-canine bond even easier and vows to deliver on that promise through positive methods only. This is a strange case, to say the least—a situation in which two similar sports (a dog trained for competitive obedience will not have problems with rally exercises) enter into a rivalry and, looking at the numbers of participants in trials in the year 2014, the sport that self-describes as less competitive and "more fun" is winning. It is not that obedience cannot be trained using positive methods only—the example of Joanna Hewelt, who is not only a multiple national champion of Poland but also dedicated to noncoercive methods, proves this false. While multiplication of fun ("rally offers more fun!") is rally's promise, a look at the definition of the term *lifestyle sport* (Wheaton, 2004) can offer a different explanation for why people believe there is more fun in rally than in obedience.

The use of the word *sport* itself to talk about these human-canine activities is significant. In Poland, *sport* was rarely used in close proximity to the term *dog training* prior to the 21st century. Training was rather seen as something of a duty: the painstaking, laborious, and sometimes unpleasant process of making the dog a useful member of human society. The word *sport* creates associations of shaping healthy bodies and healthy minds; of socially useful yet enjoyable activity; of building character through self-imposed discipline. *Sport* (applied to dog training) has appeared alongside the changes in types of training endeavors, methods applied, and stated goals of the activity. It seems that canine performance events could be classified as "lifestyle sports" because they are not all highly competitive in nature and are based on a definition of *sport* that differs from the one which emphasizes individual achievement. In the case of canine performance sports (although there is still insufficient empirical research), it seems that the dog's well-being and enjoyment are usually placed over and above the desire to win at all costs, at least on the level of declaration. Furthermore, it is the noncompetitive sports (or at least the ones that downplay the competitive aspect) that are most dynamically gaining in popularity.

Lifestyle sports offer an alternative to more competitive sports, and, as stated earlier, most of these new sports are heavily dominated by women. As Wheaton notes after Bourdieu (1984), many of these alternative sports (e.g., skateboarding, surfing, Frisbee) originated in 1960s North American counterculture and were later brought to Europe by American entrepreneurs

(Wheaton, 2004, p. 3). There is a certain similarity in the case of canine performance events in Poland: In addition to the fact that many of them originated in the United States and the United Kingdom, many individuals have devoted their lives to popularizing a particular sport—and the activity has turned into their livelihood—with hopes of offering "something different" from classic canine activities.

At the same time, the organization overtly dedicated to the development of canine training and well-being, the Polish Kennel Club has not become involved in promoting these new activities, possibly because they run counter to the very culture associated with the Club. Of the new sports, only three (agility, obedience, and dummy trials) are sanctioned by the Polish Kennel Club, but in all three cases there exist significant tensions between the authorities of the Club and the participants. While many of these result from the Club's management style (last-minute rule changes being just one example), the conflict between obedience competitors and Polish Kennel Club officials in 2014 reveals a misunderstanding on a much more fundamental level: It is based on different definitions of the goals of training.

After the 2014 World Championship qualifications, Polish Kennel Club authorities decided to organize an additional trial, which they called a "verification of the results." After the trial, the judge gathered all the competitors and delivered a long soliloquy that included strong criticism of the dogs' apparent joy and enthusiasm. The speech was secretly recorded by one of the participants and uploaded as a public YouTube video. According to the judge, an "old timer" with judging experience dating back to the 1980s, "a new manner of [the dog exhibiting] joy has become all too common."[5] The judge criticized the dogs precisely for being too happy and not submissive enough. The quotation above was found so outrageous among the dog sports community that it was quickly turned into a graphic meme, circulating on Facebook and gathering hundreds of likes. The competitors filed a petition to the governing body of the FCI, complaining of how they and their dogs have been mistreated by local Polish authorities.

This particular conflict stands out because canine performance sports are presented—maybe the word *marketed* could be used here—as primarily fun and only secondarily competitive. The emphasis on fun is so ubiquitous that a line like "the dogs are having too much fun" stands out glaringly. At the same time it seems there is something more to this fun than pure hedonism. The way *fun* is invoked in rule books, in advertisements, and in participants' descriptions of their experiences makes it sound almost wholesome. While this is the way fun is defined in many non-canine sports as well (where it is the challenge and the effort that account for fun), what makes canine sports a particularly interesting case study is the opposition between the old style of training (no fun for the dog) and the new style of training (all fun for the dog). The invocation of fun is thus itself a way of signaling the activity's place within the broader framework of the evolution of dog training. It should be added that contemporary social theorists and philosophers often note the ubiquity of fun in postmodern culture, speaking even of the imperative to enjoy or of "happiness as the supreme duty" (Žižek, 2008). Slavoj Žižek interprets this imperative as resulting from the superego's order to enjoy that which one has to do anyway, but it is not necessary to immerse oneself in Lacanian psychoanalysis to see that the postmodern subject is bombarded from all directions with imperatives to enjoy him- or herself. This emphasis on enjoyment in dog sports is yet another instance of how, in the new understanding of human-animal relations, the notions associated with human postmodern subjects are extended to nonhuman subjects. It becomes a guardian's duty to find activities that the dog will enjoy.

Conclusion

The goal of this chapter was to show the links between the emergence of the contemporary canine sports scene in Poland and the positive training revolution. I also set out to prove that the turn to newer and more positive methods among participants in canine events, analyzed in relation to the explicit goals of these activities (as expressed in rule books and as understood by participants), is not just an attempt to come up with less physically intrusive and more sophisticated methods of creating docile bodies serving human needs: There is a genuine desire among the trainers associated with these sports to identify and meet a dog's real psychological and physical needs. As a result, this analysis does enter into something of an "aesthetico-moral defense" of animal training, to use the category criticized by Paul Patton.

As an aside, I am aware that it is impossible to disentangle the identification of preexisting needs from the formation of new ones—from the emergence of a value system that is shared by both the animal and the human. However, it is the decision to enter into a relationship with a nonhuman other and the desire to shape that relationship as an ethical relationship that seem to be the structuring elements here; all the other decisions follow from the desire to develop this relationship with the nonhuman's best interests in mind, and this is what accounts for the qualitative change of the human-animal bond in the newer sporting events. This new relationship is primarily an affective relationship, while the old one was based (at least overtly) on different categories, usually those of utility. Adrian Franklin sees the turn to affective relations with animals as a response to the insecurities of the postmodern world (Franklin, 1999, p. 3) and from this perspective the very emergence of canine performance events is an element of what Franklin describes as the "extraordinary further growth in the range of activities associated with animals" (Franklin, 1999, p. 46).

I have also identified the canine sports scene as a symptomatically (post)modern phenomenon: related to notions of risk, individualization, and reflexivity and reflecting the postmodern plurality of ready-made templates of lifestyle choices that seem to be infinitely proliferating. The emphasis in lifestyle sports, which I have identified as a broader category into which canine sports fit, is not on individual achievement but on enjoyment of the activity. Finally, I see the proliferation of sporting events as tied to the postmodern imperative to enjoy oneself: one that caring guardians see as referring to their dogs as well, not just to themselves. In the context of Poland, it comes as no surprise that the canine performance sports scene emerged only after the transition from socialism to capitalism, which underscores the uneasy connection between consumerism and qualitative changes in the contemporary human-canine bond.

Notes

1. The performance of the team that won this particular event held on March 15, 2015, in Wałbrzych, Joanna Hewelt and her dog Tough, is available as a YouTube video on Joanna Hewelt's public profile: https://www.youtube.com/watch?v=Un3QKQajYhg [Accessed 1 May 2015].
2. The voiceover in 1991 VHS video is the exact text of Brzezicha, A. (1997). *Amatorskie szkolenie psów* [Amateur dog training]. Warsaw Poland: PWRiL. (Original work published 1973)
3. Theby, V., & Hares, M. (2010). *Agility. Sport i zabawa* [Agility: Sport and fun] (M. Jatowska, Trans.). Warsaw, Poland: Wydawnictwo RM.
4. Posted by Maria Kuncewicz on the "Kliker" Yahoo! Internet discussion group on February 4, 2004; from the author's personal collection of e-mails.
5. The YouTube video of the so-called verification trial that took place in April 2014 is uploaded to the YouTube profile of KlubObedience.pl and is publicly available at https://www.youtube.com/watch?v=I2SBdrIqI20 [Accessed 10 May 2015].

References

Beck, U. (1992). *Risk society: Towards a new modernity.* New York, NY: Sage.

Beck, U., & Beck-Gernsheim, E. (2002). *Individualization: Institutionalized individualism and its social and political consequences.* New York, NY: Sage.

Bonk, P. (2010). Przygoda, specyficzny klimat i swobodna atmosfera [Adventure, specific climate and relaxed atmosphere]. *Dog&Sport, 3*(7), 4–6.

Bourdieu, P. (1984). *Distinction: A social critique of the judgment of taste.* New York, NY: Routledge.

Brzezicha, A. (1980). VIII Mistrzostwa Polski Psów Obrończych [8th Polish Protection Dog Championships]. *Pies, 1*(165), 14.

Brzezicha, A. (1991). *Amatorskie szkolenie psów* [Amateur dog training; VHS video]. Warsaw, Poland: Classic.

Bukład, E. (2010). Historia oddziału krakowskiego Związku Kynologicznego w Polsce. [History of the Krakow branch of the Polish Kennel Club]. Retrieved from http://www.zkwpkrakow.pl/Historia/1.htm [Accessed 23 May 2015].

Café Animal. (2010, April 1). Agility czyli sport i zabawa [Agility that is both sport and fun] [Book review]. Retrieved from http://www.cafeanimal.pl/artykuly/zajrzyj-do-ksiazki/Vivianne-Theby-Michaela-Hares-Agility-Sport-i-zabawa-Wydawnictwo-RM,2417 [Accessed 23 May 2015].

Coppinger, R., & Coppinger, L. (2001). *Dogs: A new understanding of canine origin, behavior, and evolution.* Chicago, IL: University of Chicago Press.

Eaton, B. (2008). *Dominance in dogs: Fact or fiction?* Wenatcheee, WA: Dogwise Publishing.

Farrell, J., Hope, A., Hulstein, R., & Spaulding, S. (2015). Dog-sport competitors: What motivates people to participate with their dogs in sporting events? *Anthrozoos: A Multidisciplinary Journal of the Interactions of People & Animals, 28*(1), 61–71.

Fédération Cynologique Internationale. (2012a). *Agility regulations of the Fédération Cynologique Internationale.* Retrieved from http://www.fci.be/medias/AGI-REG-en-479.pdf [Accessed 23 May 2015].

Fédération Cynologique Internationale. (2012b). *General regulations for participation in Obedience trials and competitions in the International Obedience Class with C.A.C.I.O.B.* Retrieved from http://www.fci.be/medias/OBE-REG-CACIOB-en-484.pdf [Accessed 10 January 2016].

Franklin, A. (1999). *Animals and modern cultures. A sociology of human-animal relations in* modernity. London, UK: Sage.

Giddens, A. (1991). *Modernity and self identity.* Cambridge, UK: Polity Press

Giddens, A. (1994). *Beyond left and right: The future of radical politics.* Cambridge, UK: Polity Press.

Haraway, D. (2003). *Companion species manifesto: Dogs, people and significant otherness.* Chicago, IL: Prickly Paradigm Press.

Haraway, D. (2007). *When species meet.* Minneapolis: University of Minnesota Press.

Hewelt, J. (2013). Methodology. Retrieved from http://obediencekurs.pl/metodologia/ [Accessed 23 May 2015].

Hewelt, J. (2014). Obedience. Część 1. Samokontrola. [Obedience: Part 1—Self-control]. *Dog&Sport,* 1(2014), 20–22.

Hultsman, W. Z. (2012). Couple involvement in serious leisure: Examining participation in dog agility. *Leisure Studies, 31*(2), 231–253. http://dx.doi.org/10.1080/02614367.2011.619010

Koski, L. & Bäcklund, P. (2015). On the fringe: The positions of dogs in Finnish dog training culture. *Society & Animals, 23*(1), 24–44. http://dx.doi.org/10.1163/15685306-12341342

Lyotard, J. F. (1984). *The postmodern condition: A report on knowledge* (Vol. 10). Minneapolis: University of Minnesota Press.

Miklósi, A. (2009). *Dog behaviour, evolution and cognition.* Oxford, UK: Oxford University Press.

Patton, P. (2003). Language, power and the training of horses. In C. Wolfe (Ed.), *Zoontologies: The question of the animal* (pp. 83–99). Minneapolis: University of Minnesota Press.

Pręgowski, M. P. (2015). Your dog is your teacher: Contemporary dog training beyond radical behaviorism. *Society & Animals, 23*(6), 525–543. http://dx.doi.org/10.1163/15685306-12341383

Radomski, D. (2010). Od zera do wizjonera. *Dog&Sport* 2(6), pp. 5–6.

Rally-O Association. (2015). *Regulamin Rally Obedience Polska* [Regulations of Rally Obedience Poland]. Retrieved from http://rally-o.pl/strona_regulamin.html [Accessed 23 May 2015].

Skinner, B. F. (1938). *The behavior of organisms.* New York, NY: Appleton-Century-Crofts.

Skinner, B. F. (1976). *Beyond freedom and dignity.* New York, NY: Penguin Books. (Original work published 1971)

SKOP. (2014). *Regulamin SKOP. Sprawdzian kompetencji zespołów tropienia użytkowego* [Mantrailing Teams Competencies Test]. Retrieved from http://alteri.pl/Szkolenia-treser-psow/SKOPregulamin2014.pdf [Accessed 23 May 2015].

Stenzel, D. (2012, July 21). Tak potrafi może 5 zespołów na świecie [Maybe 5 teams in the world can do this]. Retrieved from http://www.tvn24.pl/pomorze,42/tak-potrafi-moze-5-zespolow-na-swiecie,266254.html [Accessed 23 May 2015].

Teodorowicz, A., & Woźniewicz–Dobrzyńska, M. (2014). Sport and recreational activity with a dog: Psychosocial significance of dog ownership. In F. Dias, S. Oliveria, J. Kosmaczewska, & A. Pereira (Eds.), *New trends in tourism research: A Polish perspective* (pp. 296–309). Peniche, Portugal: GITUR.

Urban, M. (2012). Rally-O, czyli sportowa współpraca [Rally-O or sporty cooperation]. *Mój Pies, 9/212*(252), 4.

Wheaton, B. (2004). *Understanding lifestyle sport: Consumption, identity and difference.* New York, NY: Routledge.

Włodarczyk, J. (2014). Strefy kontaktu, strefy władzy. Feministyczna analiza relacji kobiet i psów w sportach kynologicznych w Polsce. [Contact zones, power zones: A feminist analysis of women and dogs in canine performance sports in Poland]. In M. P. Pręgowski & J. Włodarczyk (Eds.), *Pies też człowiek? Relacje ludzi i psów we współczesnej Polsce* [A dog's life? On humans and canines in contemporary Poland] (pp. 113–151). Gdańsk, Poland: WN Katedra.

Žižek, S. (2009). *In defense of lost causes.* New York, NY: Verso.

Związek Kynologiczny w Polsce. (1979). *Regulamin szkolenia, egzaminów i zawodów psa towarzyszącego i psa obrończego* [Regulations of training, exams and competitions for companion dogs and protection dogs]. Warsaw, Poland: ZKwP.

Związek Kynologiczny w Polsce. (2007). *Regulamin prób i konkursów pracy psów myśliwskich* [Regulations of trials and competitions of hunting dogs]. Warsaw, Poland: ZKwP.

4

Dog-Assisted Therapy and Activities in Contemporary Poland

Agnieszka Wojtków

The presumption that the mere presence of other species has a positive influence on human health has a long-standing history. Contemporary, systematic interest in animals in the therapeutic context (and dogs in particular) dates back to the 1960s in the West and to the mid-1990s in Poland. This chapter presents the rise and the first decades of dog-assisted therapy in the Third Republic. It is written from the perspective of a practitioner who worked in the dog-assisted therapy field from 2006 until 2013 and whose data collection predominantly involved personal communication and participant observation in person and online.

In this chapter I look at the specificity and specialties, at times truly unique, of Polish *dogoterapia* (dog-assisted therapy, or "dogotherapy") and *kynoterapia* (cynotherapy). The chapter also covers local pitfalls and controversies, including the early split in the community stemming from the emergence of two aforementioned, competing names back in the 1990s. My work further describes the unfortunate consequences of said discord, including the lack of countrywide standards of animal-assisted activities (AAA) and animal-assisted therapy (AAT), as well as lack of consensus with regard to the recent legal establishment of the professions of *kynoterapeuta* (cynotherapist) and *dogoterapeuta* ("dogotherapist"). At the same time, by looking at the growing pains of the Polish AAA/AAT community, I aim to answer a few more universal questions, such as why establishing national standards is a necessity, and why treating dog-assisted therapy as a full-time profession is potentially hazardous to both people and dogs.

History of Animal-Assisted Therapy: An Outline

The institutional implementation of what was later dubbed animal-assisted therapy (AAT) dates back at least 200 years. Greiffenhagen and Buck-Werner (2009) mention how an 18th-century Quaker facility for the mentally ill kept a number of domestic animals precisely so that the patients would be able to take care of them. In a similar way, many late 19th-century German institutions, such as the center for epileptics in Bielefeld, kept dogs, cats, sheep, and goats to support the therapy and recovery of their patients. Such traces of therapeutic activities involving animals were never thoroughly documented, however, and therefore are not considered to be official or confirmed cases of the positive impact of animals on patients (Greiffenhagen & Buck-Werner, 2009, p. 14).

The first documented cases of the intentional use of animals in a therapeutic context date back to 1942, when the American Red Cross and the U.S. Army Air Corps established a special program dedicated to recuperating soldiers struggling with post-traumatic stress disorder. The Army Air Force Convalescent Hospital in Pawling, New York, was the place where veterans were involved in repeated interactions with a wide variety of farm animals, including cattle and horses. Interacting with these animals was part of their therapy, aimed at providing quietude and peace after emotionally difficult sessions (Bustad, 1980). However, it was not until the 1960s and the publication of Boris Levinson's *Pet-Oriented Child Psychotherapy* that a careful investigation of the therapeutic benefits of interactions with animals took place. Levinson, the author of the term *pet-facilitated therapy,* presented extensive records from his psychological practice and maintained that the fundamental role of the animal in therapy is to build a bridge between the patient and the therapist, and further between the patient and other people. The psychiatrist's own dog, Jingles, played such a role in his therapeutic work with children (Levinson, 1969). Levinson's ideas were further developed by fellow psychiatrists, including Samuel A. Corson and Elizabeth O'Leary Corson from Ohio State University. They were among the first to research and evaluate pet-facilitated therapy; they also contributed to the field by initiating the use of animals in the rehabilitation of prisoners in the United States. Pet-facilitated therapy gained particular momentum with the establishment of the Delta Foundation, later renamed Delta Society. The organization was founded in the United States in 1977 by veterinarians R. K. Anderson, Stanley Diesch, William McCulloch, and Leo K. Bustad and psychiatrist Michael McCulloch. Bustad, a professor and once dean of the College of Veterinary Medicine at Washington State University and the author of *Animals, Aging and the Aged* (1980), served as Delta's first president, from 1981 to 1988. Under him and his successors, Delta—since 2012 known as Pet Partners—has established a set of standards for pet-facilitated therapy. It has also developed a widely known nomenclature that differentiates interactions and encounters with animals (animal-assisted activities, AAA) from goal-oriented and thoroughly planned therapy (animal-assisted therapy, AAT). As the organization's primer described in 2014:

> Animal-Assisted Activities are basically the casual "meet and greet" activities that involve pets visiting people. The same activity can be repeated with many people, unlike a therapy program that is tailored to a particular person or medical condition.... AAT is a goal-directed intervention directed and/or delivered by a health/human service professional with specialized expertise, and within the scope of practice of his/her profession. AAT is designed to promote improvement in human physical, social, emotional, and/or cognitive functioning. (Pet Partners, 2014)

Organizing visits to nursing homes, schools, preschools, hospitals, orphanages, and so forth therefore fits the AAA category, whereas tailor-made programs supporting the treatment of patients with autism,

Down syndrome, and cerebral palsy, as well as aiming at improving the long-term development of children from dysfunctional families, are all good examples of AAT. Delta Society should also be credited with underlining that AAA/AAT animals are not therapists themselves and do not possess unique therapeutic skills by nature (something unfortunately still attributed to some species, particularly dolphins). Instead, animals serve as catalysts: By interacting with them, patients gain motivation to act and/or to cooperate with the therapist. Therefore animals can indirectly improve the effectiveness of the therapeutic process (Hirtenfelder, 2007, p. 84).

Numerous organizations devoted to human-animal interactions, such as, for example, the Society for Companion Animal Studies (SCAS; United Kingdom) and the Institute for Interdisciplinary Research on the Human-Pet Relationship (IEMT; Austria), were established in the West in the late 1970s and throughout the 1980s. In 1992, representatives from numerous organizations decided to turn their working relationship into an umbrella-type association, thus forming the International Association of Human-Animal Interaction Organizations (IAHAIO). The work of IAHAIO further clarified and standardized the use of animals in the therapeutic context, as well as the use of service dogs—that is, dogs assisting people with disabilities (Hirtenfelder, 2007).

Dogoterapia and *Kynoterapia* as Rival Terms in Poland: A Brief History

Considering that the restoration of democracy and the establishment of the free market economy happened in Poland merely a quarter-century ago (1989), one can say that the interest in AAT developed rather quickly. Unsurprisingly, the main focus was predominantly on dogs. Maria Czerwińska, the person widely recognized as the precursor of pet-facilitated therapy in Poland, is best known as the founder and president of *Fundacja Przyjaźni Ludzi i Zwierząt "Cze-ne-ka"* (Foundation for Human and Animal Friendship "Cze-ne-ka," established in 1998). Czerwińska had been training animals for movies for many years when in 1987 she began to occasionally take her dog companions to visit people with disabilities. She soon noticed the positive impact her dogs had on the people they visited—or, to be precise, she observed how the mere presence of her own dogs sparked positive emotions all around and how interactions with animals were a nice break in the daily routines of disabled persons. The first patients who interacted with Czerwińska's dogs were from the Educational Centre for Blind Children in Laski, in the suburbs of Warsaw.

In 1996, Czerwińska coined the term *dogoterapia* (dog-assisted therapy; direct translation: dog therapy) to describe all or most activities taking place between her dogs and patients. Whereas the introduction of the terms *pet-facilitated therapy, animal-assisted activities,* and *animal-assisted therapy* did not stir much controversy in Anglo-Saxon countries, this was not the case in Poland. The term *dogoterapia* used by Czerwińska raised some doubts from the beginning due to a rather atypical combination of words: the English *dog* and the Polish *terapia.* If a Polish prefix does not fit a newly created term well, a Latin or Greek one is typically used. This is perhaps why, even though *dogoterapia* is commonly known these days, numerous organizations use their own terms. *Kynoterapia* (cynotherapy), promoted by *Polskie Towarzystwo Kynoterapeutyczne* (PTK; Polish Society for Cynotherapy), is a particularly popular alternative, created precisely as an effort to replace *dogoterapia* for linguistic reasons. The prefix *kyno-* (or *cyno-*) comes from Greek and thus can be seen as more adequate. PTK defines *kynoterapia* as a method of enhancing the effectiveness of personality development, education, and rehabilitation, wherein a carefully selected and trained dog serves as a motivator and the whole process is conducted by a qualified cynotherapist (Polskie Towarzystwo Kynoterapeutyczne, 2014). Furthermore, some organizations do not shy away from creating their own definitions and nomenclature and come up with definitions often simply to support their own ideas about how animals can facilitate development and rehabilitation, including what the word *therapy* entails. In this fashion, for example, *Stowarzyszenie Terapii Kontaktowej z Udziałem Psów* (Association for Contact Therapy Involving Dogs) replaced the words *dogoterapia* and *kynoterapia* with *terapia kontaktowa z udziałem zwierząt* ("contact therapy with the participation of animals"). There is no doubt, however, that *dogoterapia* and *kynoterapia* are best known, a fact reflected also in legal regulations.

Similarly to other countries, Poland has managed to establish organizations aimed at the unification of rules and definitions of pet-facilitated therapy, and dog-assisted therapy in particular. The first of such organizations was *Polski Związek Dogoterapii* (PZD; Polish Dogotherapy Association), founded in 2004. Its member organizations focused on efforts to reach an agreement on the establishment of uniform methods of working with therapy dogs, therapy dog training, and the necessary qualifications of the people involved. Unfortunately, some of the PZD members were not entirely supportive of adhering to the standards promoted by the Delta Society, including its definitions of AAA and AAT. Due to the discord, some of the organizations left PZD and founded *Polskie Towarzystwo Kynoterapeutyczne* (PTK) in 2006. After merely a decade, the only trace of PZD's existence is its entry in the National Court Register, and the standards of Delta Society/Pet Partners, although still promoted by numerous organizations, are not unanimously accepted in Poland.

At the same time, PTK made efforts to define dog-assisted therapy and its standards on its own terms. In 2010, it was the driving force behind the legal establishment of the professions of *kynoterapeuta* (cynotherapist) and *dogoterapeuta* ("dogotherapist"), which were then entered into the classification of professions and specialties of the Polish Ministry of Labour and Social Policy. PTK aimed at establishing countrywide standards, as well as at preparing officially binding exams for prospective therapists and their dogs. This critically important objective, however, still has not been achieved, partly due to PTK's drive to be the dominant player rather than to cooperate with other well-established and experienced entities. This has enhanced the difficulty of reaching a crucial consensus with regard to what the canine and human exams should entail, and who should assess them. The overall result is therefore largely ambiguous: The existence of the profession is a fact, but the lack of cross-organizational standards leads to a free-for-all type of situation. For this reason, the professionalization of cynotherapy has been widely criticized by some activists, volunteers, and entities involved in AAA and AAT. The reasons for this criticism are presented later in this chapter.

Major Organizations and Contributors to the AAA/AAT Field in Poland

As previously mentioned, the short history of dog-assisted therapy in Poland can be tracked back to the establishment of *Fundacja Przyjaźni Ludzi i Zwierząt "Cze-ne-ka"* (Foundation for Human and Animal Friendship "Cze-ne-ka") in 1998. However, the existence of this organization was preceded by a different *"Cze-ne-ka"*: a dog sport club for sled dogs enthusiasts. Maria Czerwińska, herself a breeder of Alaskan Malamutes and Samoyeds, had been involved in the club before developing the idea to establish the foundation with fellow admirers of sled dogs. Her devotion to these dogs is reflected in the foundation's goals and objectives and stated on the official website (www.czeneka.org), where promoting *dogoterapia* goes hand in hand with the promotion and organization of sled dog camps and races. The abundance of photographs documenting these camps and races also seems to indicate the current priority of *"Cze-ne-ka."*

A tighter focus on dog-assisted therapy is maintained by the *Fundacja Pomocy Osobom Niepełnosprawnym "Przyjaciel"* (Foundation for People With Disabilities "Friend"), established in the capital city of Warsaw in 2002 and thriving in its second decade of existence. Its mission includes popularizing dog-assisted therapy; preparing therapists to conduct meetings and sessions; educating children and youth with regard to safe interactions with dogs; activating disabled and elderly persons; educating parents and guardians; and raising public awareness of the difficulties of people with disabilities. The Foundation's website (www.przyjaciel.pl) lists key activities offered to the public: therapeutic sessions in the form of individual meetings (usually for children with disabilities and those fearing dogs); educational activities for preschool and school groups; and birthday parties involving dogs. A pivotal contribution of the organization is that it has published numerous books on dog-assisted therapy and activities and provides ready-made scenarios for therapy sessions or education-related meetings (cf. Fundacja Pomocy Osobom Niepełnosprawnym Przyjaciel, 2008).

A similar educative approach was taken by *Fundacja Dogtor* (The Dogtor Foundation). This organization, based in Gdynia, Poland, and founded in 2003 by Marta Lichnerowicz, nowadays specializes in organizing seminars for people wanting to get started in the field of dog-assisted therapy. *Dogtor* is also involved in the dog training field and promotes AAA and AAT through participation in local and countrywide outdoor events and social campaigns. The year 2003 also saw the birth of the *Ama Canem Foundation* (first led by Andrzej Niedzielski and later by Małgorzata Stankiewicz), as well as of *Cane Pro Humano Foundation*, both involved in the establishment of PZD in 2004. Another notable organization with a relatively long history is the Warsaw-based *Fundacja Razem Łatwiej—Zwierzęta przełamują bariery* (It's Easier Together—Animals Break Barriers Foundation), founded in 2005 and devoted to promoting Delta Society standards as well as felinotherapy (i.e., therapeutic activities involving the presence of cats). Its members have also developed a pioneering program supporting palliative treatments in one of Warsaw's hospices. A similar idea of external cooperation in order to support the well-being of patients was developed by *Stowarzyszenie Zwierzęta Ludziom* (Animals for Humans Association), registered in 2008 and known for its pilot program with the Children's Memorial Health Institute, the largest and most modern specialist pediatric hospital in Poland. Another pioneering organization, *Fundacja Edukacyjna "Pies i Staś"* (Educational Foundation "Dog and Staś," established in 2006 under a slightly different name), developed its own specialized field within Polish dog-assisted therapy, turning its focus to children from socially challenged and dysfunctional families. Over the years *"Pies i Staś"* has established numerous programs in what it calls *dogoterapia społeczna* (social dogotherapy). The organization also focuses on promoting dog bite prevention in schools and preschools, as well as organizing seminars and workshops on these topics.

In the second decade of the 21st century, Poland is home to dozens of entities involved in dog-assisted therapy and activities. At the same time, standardization of the practices remains a glaring issue.

Despite a nearly 20-year history of dog-assisted therapy in Poland, the country lacks cross-organizational agreement with regard to who can visit clients and patients with a dog (and under which circumstances, when, and how).[1] Many of the organizations adhere to the standards established by the Delta Society/Pet Partners, including standards relating to acceptable and unacceptable working conditions for dogs. Delta's guidelines, as well as its

The *"Pies i Staś"* foundation developed its own specialization within Polish dog-assisted therapy, turning the focus to children from socially challenged and dysfunctional families. This nongovernmental organization also focuses on promoting dog bite prevention in schools and preschools. (Photo by Michał Piotr Pręgowski.)

essential division (AAA and AAT), have been promoted—for example, by *Dogtor* and *Razem Łatwiej—Zwierzęta przełamują bariery*, as well as *"Pies i Staś."* As mentioned previously, other entities, including PTK, came up with their own definitions. Some people involved in the field believe the lack of understanding started with the creation of two terms, *dogoterapia* and *kynoterapia*, something they see as the beginning of a far-reaching split covering many aspects of work in a patient-dog-therapist triad. Although the number of Polish organizations involved in dog-assisted therapy is rather significant, few of them cooperate closely today—perhaps due to early misunderstandings and conflicts in the community.

At the same time, some precursors of *dogoterapia* and *kynoterapia* are being questioned by other members of the community for promoting methods and activities that do not have measurable educational or therapeutic impact on the patient, and may even pose a danger to the dogs or patients involved. The significant advances in knowledge about the effects of AAT, as well as about canine and feline behavior and physiology, often elude the practitioners. The key complaints voiced in personal communication and/or expressed in online discussions can be categorized as follows:

- Excessive focus on maintaining close physical contact between the patient and the dog, including frequent stroking, hugging, embracing, and lying down on the animal, passing under or over the animal, and grooming
- Erroneous understanding of the general idea of dog-assisted therapy, perceived as a very direct involvement of the dog in sessions with patients, and focused on activities such as those mentioned in the first bulleted point
- Inadequate preparation of dogs chosen to participate in therapeutic and/or educational sessions, lack of verification of their skills, and exposing them to uncomfortable, health-threatening interactions with patients

It should be noted that many organizations gather enthusiasts passionate about AAA/AAT who are focused on keeping up with the academic knowledge as well as understanding dog behavior and physiology. Such people readily adjust their approach in order to preserve the well-being of both the patient and the animal. Unfortunately, newcomers are educated as much by the "old timers" who simply "know their ways" as they are by the "geeks" fascinated by canine science, thus are prone to adopting bad habits and having a misguided concept of what to expect from their animals in the AAA/AAT context. Moreover, along with the establishment of the cynotherapist/dogotherapist profession in 2010, both individuals and companies can offer their services in the field of dog-assisted therapy—all without having to adhere to a set of countrywide standards due to their nonexistence.

Indications and Contraindications for AAT: The Polish Perspectives

The early focus of dog-assisted therapy in Poland was predominantly on working with people with disabilities. The late 1990s and early 2000s saw the publishing of the first Polish articles and books aimed at sharing preliminary experiences, as well as presenting therapeutic programs designed to work with clients, particularly those with Down syndrome, cerebral palsy, and autism. The emphasis was often put on different roles canines play depending on the therapeutic context; for example, in the case of patients with autism, dogs usually serve as facilitators of contact established between the therapist and the patient, whereas in the therapy of children with cerebral palsy, dogs often play the role of motivators and help diversify the predominantly monotonous exercises (Kałużyńska, 2003, p. 33). The therapy for patients with Down syndrome, in turn, includes dog-related exercises with the goal of, for example, increasing the efficiency of the patients' circulatory and respiratory systems (Rybacka, 2003, p. 37). More general indications for inclusion of dog-assisted therapy in the treatment include

- intellectual, physical and sensory disabilities;
- low social functioning;
- imbalance of the nervous system;
- emotional and mental disorders; and
- somatic disability (when physical and mental efficiency is decreased due to somatic diseases such as cancer, diabetes or multiple sclerosis) (Trofimov, 2010, p. 10).

A few Polish authors have described the usefulness of dog-assisted therapy in their personal work. Marzena Machoś-Nikodem (2007), a speech therapist, discusses the application of AAT for treating speech disorders; her work aims at improving verbal and nonverbal communication and stimulating children's' spontaneous communication activity. A dog's mere presence, as well as simple activities performed with the patient, are woven into the broader program designed to stimulate the tactile system (one that includes controlled physical contact with the animal), as well as to improve the work of the articulatory organs and/or to support learning how to read (Machoś-Nikodem, 2007, p. 11). Dog-assisted therapy is also very useful in psychopedagogical therapy efforts in Poland, as described by the authors of the collective work titled *Terapia psychopedagogiczna z udziałem psa* (Psychopedagogical therapy with dogs), edited by Monika Włodarczyk-Dudka (2006). Such therapy entails psychological, pedagogical, and logopedic means oriented toward the causes and symptoms present in children with, for example, learning difficulties and speech impediments; psychopedagogical therapy then aims to eliminate patient's failures, and the negative consequences of such failures, from the learning process (Włodarczyk-Dudka, 2006, p. 21).

The contraindications for the use of dog-assisted therapy are also the focus of many Polish practitioners. However, gaining knowledge goes hand in hand with getting more experience; therefore, in the first decade or so, the most acknowledged contraindication was allergy to animal hair and dander, as well as asthma (Popławska, 2003, p. 20). Over the years, local awareness of the complexities of dog-assisted therapy has risen significantly, and issues such as infectious diseases, eczema, lesions and rashes, diabetes, severe mental illness, and open wounds, as well as postsurgical convalescence of the patient and his or her potential fear of dogs, are now recognized. Such recognition of contraindications mirrors that discussed in the German literature (cf. Greiffenhagen & Buck-Werner, 2009; Röger-Lakenbrink, 2006). Additional contraindications include the lack of consent on the client's side (including the consent of his or her guardians), as well as the client's aggressive behavior toward the therapy dog, effectively putting the animal's well-being, safety, and/or health at risk.

Contemporary Challenges for *Dogoterapia* and *Kynoterapia* in Poland

As is the case in numerous other countries, dog-assisted therapy is an attractive topic for the Polish mass media. Journalists gladly present success stories of people who reached a therapy or rehabilitation breakthrough thanks to interacting with therapy animals. By disregarding the complexity of factors involved, and focusing primarily on the subjective feelings of the parents or guardians (i.e., people who are the most emotionally invested in the breakthrough), mass media reinforce a misguided perception of AAT and its effectiveness. The improvements seen in patients could, for example, stem merely from the stimulatory influence of an exciting change in the routine—and in many cases the "revolutionary improvement" seen after sessions with therapy dogs could be maintained by a systematic replacement of the stimuli, so that the patient would be immersed in exciting and novel experiences for a prolonged period. Journalists also do not pay attention to the durability of changes, the most important part in the evaluation of the effectiveness of any treatment. This weakness is extremely important, especially if we follow Hal Herzog's hesitation and observe how little quantitative research has been performed to prove the long-term effects of AAT in relation to various dysfunctions (Herzog, 2011).

Aside from dealing with exaggerated public expectations, Polish practitioners struggle with delivering a clear vision as to what dog-assisted therapy entails. As previously mentioned, in 2010, due to the efforts of the PTK, the Polish Ministry of Labour and Social Policy officially registered dog-assisted therapy as a profession. It was placed among "technicians and other middle-level personnel," in subgroup no. 323, "Practitioners of Unconventional or Complementary Therapy Methods," under the number 323007 and the name *kynoterapeuta (dogoterapeuta)* (cynotherapist [dogotherapist]). However, the establishment of the profession has not solved the biggest problem in Polish dog-assisted therapy: the lack of countrywide standards regarding the work of therapeutic teams (which should, but often do not, consist of a therapist, a dog, and either the handler or a therapist's assistant if the therapist is the handler). No national guidelines have yet been established as to who can conduct sessions, what type of education they should have, or how to prepare dogs for their future involvement in AAA or AAT.

National standards are vital, especially with regard to participating dogs, as the lack of guidelines and proper control may lead to animal abuse. Many organizations are aware of short-term and long-term risks associated with overstressing therapy animals and adhere to self-imposed limits when working with them (such as working less than two hours a day, and often an hour every two days, with a single dog). The latter is also a good example of the "animal turn" observed in the Polish AAT community in the last few years; however, recognizing animal welfare issues as inherent to dog-assisted therapy is not yet common, and a countrywide discussion regarding canine well-being in *kynoterapia* and *dogoterapia* has yet to take place.

The importance of a handler's knowledge of dogs, their behavior and physiology, is also important for the client's safety. A handler's ignorance may lead to undesirable or even dangerous behaviors presented by a stressed animal during a session. If the worst-case scenario—a Polish patient severely bitten by a dog—was to materialize, it would inevitably attract the attention of tabloids and other sensation-seeking entities, possibly staining the reputation of the whole AAT community in Poland. Such fear has prompted some organizations to be particularly proactive and to establish their own organizational standards. These usually apply to both people and dogs, requiring both groups to pass internal exams before they are allowed to work with clients and patients. Such organizational regulations also dictate how to prepare particular sessions and what formal education is required to work as a therapist (e.g., those without a master's degree in pedagogy, special pedagogy, or education can still contribute as dog handlers or assistants, but they cannot conduct the sessions). Such standards may also define what a given person needs to learn, especially in the field of dog behavior and dog training. Some organizations also suggest how to choose and prepare dogs for future work.

Dogoterapia and the Canine Issues

The establishment of the *kynoterapeuta (dogoterapeuta)* profession raised doubts in the AAT community almost from the beginning. Some questioned whether such registration was at all needed and were not happy with how dog-assisted therapy became unambiguously associated with salaried work. The mere fact of charging money for dog-assisted sessions was not problematic—even though the vast majority of Polish practitioners work nonprofit, they often accept donations to cover the operational costs and/or to invest in their own and their dog's development. The source of controversy was the profession itself, and the implication that a person can make dog-assisted therapy his or her main source of income, working full-time with a dog or a few dogs.

In the opinion of many members of the AAT community (particularly those involved in dog training as well, thus more knowledgeable about canine behavior and physiology), having to work 9 to 5, five days a week, together with the pressures of professional obligations, could easily lead to disregarding the welfare of the dog. If we agree that the lack of stability in the environment, constantly changing places and being exposed to new stimuli (including, but not being limited to, meeting new people), as well as being exposed to numerous distractions, are in general far from desirable for dogs—we will end up concluding that they cannot be treated like full-time employees or coworkers. Moreover, since most therapy dogs are expected to perform (i.e., respond to certain commands) to some extent, one should consider that their performance would likely be influenced negatively in a situation of prolonged stress, when their cortisol levels are elevated (see also Miklósi, 2009).

The solution, of course, could be to have several therapy dogs and to work with them interchangeably, thus providing each animal with enough relaxation and downtime. However, preparing a dog to work in dog-assisted therapy generates costs and, above all, requires time and commitment on the part of the human, thus making the hypothetical existence of the five-dogs-and-one-therapist team rather unlikely.

Furthermore, the readiness to participate in designed activities is also an issue. Every puppy requires months of training before being ready to meet patients or clients. On the other end, dogs at a certain age or with certain health conditions should be removed from service. Professional work usually includes signing contracts, and external obligations could easily lead to pressures, where the dog's well-being could lose its priority status. The health of the animal, in fact, is generally problematic: Would a full-time cynotherapist (dogotherapist) let his or her dog "call in sick"? There is no other option if the person adheres to international standards like the ones promoted by Pet Partners. Could the person afford to do it, though, if this is how he or she makes a living? The answers to these two questions are important for ethical reasons, but there are safety issues involved as well.

Another issue revolves around breed stereotypes. This problem is surely international. Some dog breeds, such as Labrador Retrievers, Golden Retrievers, and Cavalier King Charles Spaniels, are dubbed particularly predisposed to dog-assisted therapy. Although dispelling such myths is not the aim of this article, it is worth mentioning that sometimes the stereotypes regarding breed predispositions come from the dog-assisted therapy community itself and/or are reinforced by some of its members. A good example from Poland involves three sled dog breeds—Alaskan Malamute, Siberian Husky, and Samoyed—all labeled as "perfect therapy dogs" and largely overrepresented in the local AAT community in its early days. The overrepresentation of these breeds tracks back to the establishment of the *"Cze-ne-ka"* foundation, whose members were also admirers of these breeds. Unfortunately, the notion that sled dogs are particularly predisposed for therapeutic work was disseminated by the mass media, effectively reinforcing the misunderstanding and influencing the popularity of these breeds in Poland. To this day some breeders advertise their sires and dams by exhibiting their therapeutic past (be it incidental), subsequently implying their dogs' unique and flawless characters. For many people who plan to get involved in dog-assisted therapy, as well as for parents of children with a disability, choosing puppies born from "perfect parents" is often imperative. In fact, in the last decade or so, numerous families of such children have bought Alaskan Malamutes, Huskies, and Samoyeds with high hopes and often very little knowledge with regard to the actual needs of these dogs. According to Austrian professor Irene Sommerfeld-Stur, the claim that some breeds have a genetic predisposition for therapy is unauthorized and not supported by scientific evidence (cf. Röger-Lakenbrink, 2006). Many dog lovers and therapists are not aware of this; some are undoubtedly mired with the vision of the noble superiority of their favorite breed over other breeds, whereas others simply benefit from supporting the myth.

Sled dog breeds remain generally popular in Poland to this day, even though very few people participate in racing-related activities and not a lot of dog guardians are ready to devote time and space to cater to the needs of these usually very energetic canines. Fortunately their overrepresentation within the AAT community seems to be trending downward. In fact, presently only a few organizations specialize in particular breeds like

"Cze-ne-ka" does; a brief review of the official websites of the Polish AAA/AAT organizations clearly shows breed variety.[2] Aside from Labrador and Golden Retrievers, Cavalier King Charles Spaniel, and sled dogs, one can find the representatives of breeds such as Australian Shepherd, Ca de Bou, Central Asian Shepherd Dog, Bearded Collie, Borzoi, French Briard, West Highland White Terrier, Lagotto Romagnolo, Bernese Mountain Dog, Shih Tsu, and Gordon Setter. At the same time, Poland has yet to capitalize on promoting the use of dogs of mixed breeding, older dogs, rescue dogs, and other kinds of, as Kris Butler put it, "throw-away dogs" who, by some, are not viewed as good candidates for home companions (Butler, 2004, pp. 18–19). Furthermore, as therapy dogs are often praised as "smart and extremely intelligent" by the public, a better effort should be made to educate the public about the basics of canine training, which is responsible for what is mistakenly perceived as an inherited trait (Butler, 2004, p. 19).

Skeptics rightly point out that neither mating two flawless canines working in AAT nor conducting the most extensive puppy predisposition tests will ever guarantee that a buyer will end up with the perfect therapy dog. Many Poles involved in dog-assisted therapy in the second decade of the 21st century understand this very well: They no longer seek predispositions in dog pedigree and instead recognize the importance of individual characteristics and of trying to match a particular animal's traits with the tasks required. Accepting the eventuality of ending up with a dog unsuitable for work in AAA or AAT is also important, especially bearing in mind that personality traits and preferences of dogs can change in a similar way that they change in humans. Needless to say, these issues are universal rather than unique to Poles.

Conclusions: Toward a Better, Brighter Future?

The establishment of the cynotherapist (dogotherapist) profession, seen by some as proof of progress, has not yet resulted in the expected revolution in the social perception of therapy dogs and dog-assisted therapy per se. Individuals and public organizations (including, e.g., schools and preschools) have very little knowledge about the legal establishment of the cynotherapist profession and usually do not request any official credentials from visitors with dogs. As discussed earlier, the most important goal—the standardization of dog-assisted therapy definitions and understandings, as well as establishing a unified set of guidelines— so far has not been achieved. The biggest problems are therefore that, despite the fact that nearly 20 years have passed since *dogoterapia* and *kynoterapia* were established as professions, (1) therapeutic sessions can still be organized by people lacking relevant formal education and (2) dogs participating in such sessions are not always subject to careful and methodical selection. Other challenges are (3) recognizing animal welfare issues on a larger scale and (4) establishing standardized, unified exams for people wishing to work in the AAA/AAT fields.

Despite the chaos on the cross-organizational level, numerous entities work very hard to develop innovative educational and therapeutic programs and continue to raise the qualifications of their volunteers and dogs. Many organizations build on the experience of foreign experts and show great concern for the ethical aspects of animal use in dog-assisted therapy. Moreover, Polish specialists have begun to participate in international initiatives and conferences and to share good practices and ideas with others; such is the case of Gabriela Drwięga and Zofia Pietruczuk from the *Fundacja Psi Uśmiech* (Dog's Smile Foundation), who educate others at the annual International Companion Animal Welfare Conference while cooperating with a large British nongovernmental organization, Dogs Trust, on shelter dog enrichment programs in Northeastern Poland.

At the same time, a certain change in focus, from therapy to education, can be observed. Some organizations now specialize predominantly in educational programs rather than therapeutic ones. Polish primary schools and preschools are keen to organize meetings at which a human-canine team promotes better understanding of dogs. Interaction with the therapy dog is usually a pretext to share invaluable information on topics such as dog bite prevention. Such meetings are not therapeutic per se, although they require thorough planning and go significantly beyond what AAA entails. *Dogoterapia,* the umbrella term, is still readily used and will most likely remain in use by Poles—however, it seems like the accent at present is put more on *dog* and less on *terapia.*

Notes

1. In this chapter I refer to the subjects of *dogoterapia* and *kynoterapia* as both "clients" and "patients" because some interventions (AAA) are devoid of the therapeutic context (AAT). Thus, not all subjects are patients.
2. I surveyed these websites in March 2013 and then again in December 2014.

References

Bustad, L .K. (1980). *Animals, aging, and the aged.* Minneapolis: University of Minnesota Press.

Butler, K. (2004). *Therapy dogs today: Their gifts, our obligation.* Norman, UK: Funpuddle Publishing Associates.

Fundacja Pomocy Osobom Niepełnosprawnym Przyjaciel. (2008). *Czy zwierzęta potrafią leczyć?* [Can animals heal?]. Warsaw, Poland: Fundacja Pomocy Osobom Niepełnosprawnym Przyjaciel.

Greiffenhagen, S., & Buck-Werner, O. (2009). *Tiere als Therapie* [Animals and therapy]. Nerdlen, Germany: Kynos.

Herzog, H. (2011). *Some we love, some we hate, some we eat: Why it's so hard to think straight about animals.* New York, NY: Harper Perennial.

Hirtenfelder, S. (2007). *Hundephobie bei Kindern und Jugendlichen* [Dog phobia in children and adolescents]. Saarbrücken, Germany: Dr. Müller.

Kałużyńska, K. (2003). Dogoterapia w pracy z dziećmi z dziecięcym porażeniem mózgowym. [Dogotherapy in the work with children with cerebral palsy]. In N. Bekasiewicz (Ed.), *Dogoterapia. Terapia kontaktowa z udziałem psów: założenia i wykorzystywanie w pracy z osobami niepełnosprawnymi* [Dogotherapy: Contact therapy with dogs—Its goals and uses in working with the disabled] (pp. 33–36). Warsaw, Poland: Fundacja Pomocy Osobom Niepełnosprawnym Przyjaciel.

Levinson, B. M. (1969). *Pet-oriented child psychotherapy.* Springfield, IL: Charles C Thomas.

Machoś-Nikodem, M. (2007). *Dogoterapeutyczny program polisensorycznej stymulacji porozumiewania się* [Dogotherapeutic program of polysensory communication stimulation]. Warsaw, Poland: CMPPP.

Miklósi, A. (2009). *Dog behaviour, evolution and cognition*. Oxford, UK: Oxford University Press.

Pet Partners. (2014). History and founders: Delta Society, the early years. Retrieved from http://petpartners.org/document.doc?id=1102 [Accessed 23 May 2015].

Polskie Towarzystwo Kynoterapeutyczne (2014). *Standardy* [Standards]. Retrieved from http://kynoterapia.eu/standardy.html [Accessed 23 May 2015].

Popławska, A. (2003). Podstawowe założenia dogoterapii [The main goals of dogotherapy]. In N. Bekasiewicz (Ed.), *Dogoterapia. Terapia kontaktowa z udziałem psów: założenia i wykorzystywanie w pracy z osobami niepełnosprawnymi* [Dogotherapy: Contact therapy with dogs—Its goals and uses in working with the disabled] (pp. 19–26). Warsaw, Poland: Fundacja Pomocy Osobom Niepełnosprawnym Przyjaciel.

Röger-Lakenbrink, I. (2006). *Das Therapiehunde-Team* [The therapy dog team]. Mürlenbach, Germany: Kynos.

Rybacka, O. (2003). Dogoterapia w pracy z dziećmi z zespołem Downa. [Dogotherapy in working with children with Down syndrome] In N. Bekasiewicz (Ed.), *Dogoterapia. Terapia kontaktowa z udziałem psów: założenia i wykorzystywanie w pracy z osobami niepełnosprawnymi* [Dogotherapy: Contact therapy with dogs—Its goals and uses in working with the disabled] (pp. 37–40). Warsaw, Poland: Fundacja Pomocy Osobom Niepełnosprawnym Przyjaciel.

Trofimov, M. (2010). *Podstawy dogoterapii* [The basics of dogotherapy] [Educational script]. Warsaw, Poland: Fundacja Edukacyjna "Pies i Staś."

Włodarczyk-Dudka, M. (Ed.). (2006). *Terapia psychopedagogiczna z udziałem psa* [Psychopedagogical therapy with dogs]. Ostróda, Poland: Drwęca.

5

Representations of Dogs in Recent Polish Memoirs and Novels

Małgorzata Rutkowska

Though in the last decades of the 20th century dog memoirs became an accepted autobiographical subgenre on both sides of the Atlantic, such works were virtually unknown in Poland until the beginning of the 21st century. Before 1989, those few Polish authors who did write on their dogs either addressed the books to young readers[1] or created conventional sketches of favorite family pets, praising their beauty, loyalty, and sagacity.[2] The first Polish memoirs that put human relationships with dogs (and other domestic animals) in the foreground rather than the background of family life were published after 1995. Quite recently, dogs have also entered the domain of fiction, appearing as characters in popular chick lit books[3] or as narrators in novels aimed at adult rather than young readers.[4] These new literary developments indicate a certain shift—by no means dramatic but rather slow and gradual—in the perceptions and representations of dogs in Polish popular culture. Until recently, household dogs were represented primarily as watchdogs or children's pets and the relationship with them rarely went beyond master-servant dependence. At present, more and more dogs—both those depicted in literary works and those actually living in

Polish families—have come to be treated as companion animals. Some of them now occupy a position reserved so far for human members of the family. In this chapter I analyze some of these new trends in the representation of dogs and the human-canine bond in selected Polish novels and memoirs published since 1989. I read these books alongside their better known American counterparts to determine culture-specific differences in the way the human-canine relationship is experienced and shown in recent nonfiction and fiction in both countries.

As the number of dogs kept in Polish homes has considerably increased in recent years, the potential audience for fictional and nonfictional representations of the human-canine bond has also steadily grown. Publishers have already discovered this niche in the market, not only bringing out in translation a number of best-selling American dog memoirs[5] but also making the readers familiar with such classics of the genre as Virginia Woolf's *Flush* or J. R. Ackerley's *My Dog Tulip.*[6] It needs to be emphasized, however, that the size and nature of the audiences of the Polish and American book markets are hardly comparable, so in all likelihood Polish dog memoirs will never enjoy such popularity as their counterparts do in the United States. Moreover, the emergence of dog memoirs in the United States was also a consequence of a shift in autobiographical writing that occurred in the 1980s when authors traditionally excluded from autobiographical discourse—women, ethnic and sexual minorities, drug addicts, and victims of sexual abuse—began to publish their life stories (Pinsker, 2003, p. 313). A similar democratization of the autobiographical genre, which encourages "ordinary people" to share their life stories with a wide audience, has not taken place in Poland.

The Family Dog

Contemporary American dog memoirs can be interpreted as a subcategory of "relational life writing"—that is, a type of narrative in which one's life is "viewed through the lens of its relation to some other key person," most often a parent, sometimes a sibling, a friend, or a lover, functioning as "the proximate other" to the autobiographer (Eakin, 1999, p. 86). In the case of dog memoirs, the proximate other is not a person but a dog, often indeed represented as the closest "family member," friend, and confidant. While these books range in tone from the humorous to the melancholic, their authors share a conviction that the years spent in the company of exceptionally "good" or unbelievably "bad" dogs changed the course of their lives for good. Thus, in American dog memoirs the proverbial "man's best friend" often functions not only as a companion but as a teacher or even spiritual guide to his human guardian.[7]

One noticeable difference between American dog memoirs and their Polish counterparts is that the former usually present the story of a one-to-one relationship, focusing on an intimate bond between a single person and his or her special, favorite dog, while in the latter the family circle is more extended and usually includes a married couple with not just one but several domestic animals.[8] Naturally, the presence of other dogs or dogs and cats in the house changes the "home pack's" dynamics, creating opportunities for socialization and play. Interestingly, the choice to open one's home to several companion animals is deliberate. The authors of Polish dog memoirs are usually aware that even though dogs have been incorporated into a human family, they still have special social and emotional needs that must be satisfied in contact with other dogs, rather than humans. Moreover, observing the hierarchy and interactions in the home pack is not only considered a highly educational experience but also one of the greatest pleasures of dog-keeping (Fijałkowski, 2009, pp. 39–43; Sędzikowska, 2012, pp. 215–255; Szulc, 1995, p. 59).

Such a way of thinking about the human-canine bond finds its confirmation in a sociological study devoted to Polish pet guardians. According to Krzysztof Konecki (2005), Poles alternate between anthropomorphic and animalistic perspectives in their interactions with animals (pp. 42–43). In other words, a universal human tendency to perceive dogs as almost human in their intelligence, emotions, and behaviors is moderated by the willingness—more or less grounded in amateur ethological knowledge—to also acknowledge their animal nature. In American memoirs, an intense one-on-one relationship usually precludes the formation of any other emotional bonds that could rival in importance the relationship between the guardian and the animal companion. The dog who is represented as the guardian's mirror is neither expected nor encouraged to act on his natural canine interests or desires.[9]

Interspecies Communication

The rationale behind all dog memoirs is similar: It stems from the author's conviction that he or she can understand what the dog communicates with a gaze, gestures, postures, and attitudes. For some, such rapport starts in childhood; Dorota Sumińska and Ewa Szulc both attribute their lifelong passion for dogs to childhood experiences. Growing up as the only children and being of frail health, they each pined for a sibling or a playmate and were eventually given dogs to make them feel less lonely. The chance to study dog behavior and body language sparked their interest in the world of animal minds and emotions and taught them the basic rules of harmonious human-animal cooperation. In her autobiography titled *Autobiografia na czterech łapach, czyli historia jednej rodziny oraz psów, kotów, krów, koni, jeży, słoni, węży … i ich krewnych* (A four-footed autobiography or a story of one family and its dogs, cats, cows, horses, hedgehogs, elephants, snakes … and their relatives),[10] Sumińska recollects Wiwa, a beloved companion of her lonely childhood who taught her how to love: "She was my sister, my friend and my hot-water bottle" (Sumińska, 2008, p. 125). This relationship was so important that it influenced her future career as she decided to become a veterinarian.[11]

In *Kto tu szczeka?* (Who is barking?), Ewa Szulc pays tribute to Nora, a three-year-old Irish setter her family adopted when she was a child, stating that she was "a friend, a partner and a teacher of dog language, dog needs, dog *savoir-vivre* and *savoir-faire*" (Szulc, 1995, p. 11). When, after many years, Szulc read Konrad Lorenz's books on dogs, she was surprised that his observations were considered groundbreaking:

> It seemed to me that every dog guardian should know all that because his own dog must have told him, showed him and taught him. Well, not every dog has such ambitions to educate his human

> as Nora had and perhaps few guardians want to listen to what the dog wants to communicate. (Szulc, p. 23)

Those who do want to listen—and the authors of dog books claim they understand what their dogs communicate to them—also wish to pass on what they have learned to readers navigating their way between incomprehension of animal otherness and reductive anthropomorphization. As Mark Doty (2008) puts it in *Dog Years,* we "make figures of speech ... invent metaphors to help us understand the world. To choose to live with a dog is to agree to participate in a long process of interpretation—a mutual agreement, though the human being holds most of the cards" (p. 1). "Translation" can be done in two ways: either by including imagined conversations with the dog or by making him a coauthor of the book, who narrates incidents from his own point of view. Both solutions stretch generic conventions of nonfictional narratives and both have been employed in Polish as well as American dog memoirs. In Jędrzej Fijałkowski's *Emil, czyli kiedy szczęśliwe są psy, szczęśliwy jest cały świat* (Emil, or when the dogs are happy the whole world is happy), readers find short, funny dialogues between Emil, a happy-go-lucky Great Dane, and his quick-tempered guardian, who tends to worry too much. Yet, there is also another, almost metaphysical level of human-canine communication, an understanding hard to explain rationally or verbally. Wondering what is so special about his dog, Fijałkowski (2009) writes:

> You can admire his frank muzzle and his intelligent gaze but there is more—something elusive, inexpressible and hard to measure. He emanates with warmth, not bodily warmth of a comforting dog but some internal energy. Many people deny its existence while others experience it in their daily encounters. (p. 73)

To be able to communicate with Emil, a human needs to discover a similar sensitivity in himself. Evoking a New Age concept of a new era, Fijałkowski predicts, half-jokingly, that once it begins, Emil will surely be reincarnated as some kind of a noble guru.

In general, there are two groups of dogs that end up having their "biographies" written: the perfect ones and the bad ones, who are, nevertheless, paradoxically good. Joanna Sędzikowska's intelligent, energetic, and mischievous Alaskan Malamutes, Raptor, Inka, and Luna—the main protagonists of *Psy z piekła rodem* (Hounds from hell)—resemble John Grogan's (2005) infamous Marley, "the world's worst dog." Both Sędzikowska and Grogan focus in their books on incorrigible behavior of animals who repeatedly ruin the house, garden, and social life of their guardians, yet for all their faults they are deeply loved. When they are "given a chance to speak," the Malamutes affirm their loyalty to the pack and express puzzlement at human ways. From their point of view, the guardians, whom they call the "Eskimos," have little understanding for vital dog needs like hunting live poultry or pigeons, eating carrion, or bathing in manure. They insist on daily baths and refuse to share chocolate with the dogs (Sędzikowska, 2012, p. 278). This humorous litany of complaints is conventional enough but marks an attempt to go beyond the anthropocentric perspective. Sędzikowska accepts the damages made by her Malamutes as part of the package, trying to understand and explain their behavior in terms of ethology and genetic legacy.

The dogs have always fascinated Sędzikowska, yet paradoxically it was not so much her emotional closeness to Raptor as it was the traumatic experience of Raptor being mauled by two aggressive dogs from the neighborhood that made her study the canine world. Obsessed with discovering a reason behind the attack, she began to read academic books and popular manuals on canine ethology. "I don't remember being ever so fascinated with any topic. The behavior of Raptor and other dogs became no longer puzzling but obvious and clear. I started dreaming about having my own pack. To be able to observe daily their social interactions, body language and communication, to give Raptor a chance to be a dog among other dogs" (Sędzikowska, 2012, p. 127). This dream came true when she began to foster abandoned Malamutes in her own home, working as a volunteer for *Fundacja Ochrony Malamutów* (The Foundation for the Protection of Alaskan Malamutes) and rehabilitating the dogs before adoption.

A Dog With a Past

Understanding a dog's past experiences is essential in the case of animals that experienced abuse, neglect, or starvation at human hands. In general, the nature of experiences described in Polish and American dog memoirs differs radically, because Polish guardians most often adopt mature dogs "with a past," subsequently facing many challenges connected with their physical and psychological rehabilitation. These are, invariably, dogs that urgently need to be saved: homeless, sick, starved, flea ridden, and dirty. In contrast, American dog memoirs usually open with a scene of buying a lovely, healthy puppy—a scene promising a fresh start to both sides involved in a relationship. No awareness of future behavior or health problems spoils a happy moment when a puppy and a human select each other to share a life. Naturally, some authors do write about adopted dogs, but it is a much less frequent scenario in American books.

It is interesting to compare how the guardians in Jon Katz's *A Good Dog* and Ewa Szulc's *Who Is Barking?* deal with a dog's past. Katz's (2006) memoir tells the story of Devon, a failed herding champion, whom he adopted out of pity and admiration for the breed. Devon's obedience problems most certainly have their source in the dog's training in the past, yet Katz is not interested in finding out what mistakes Devon's previous guardians may have committed. Instead, he tries to explain the dog's emotional problems in terms of his unruly and overemotional character. In her book, Szulc describes Ar, a three-year-old setter who changed hands nine times before she adopted him. As a result he became "the dog with a damaged psyche, with no free will, deprived of a joy of life or ability to play. I took a creature which resembled a manikin, a dog so obedient and deprived of initiative that it was terrifying and made our first days together a horror" (Szulc, 1995, p. 31). Though with time his psychological condition improved, for the next 13 years Ar never quite got rid of the fear inculcated in him in youth and remained unable to enjoy walks or spontaneous play with other dogs. Szulc has finally accepted that, for all her efforts to give him back the joy of life, Ar would never behave like other dogs and therefore she stopped forcing changes on him. Katz, who devoted a few years of his life to making unpredictable Devon first a good shepherd's dog and then a good pet, has never reached this point in their relationship. When all the measures failed and the dog remained unruly and occasionally aggressive, Katz's disappointment proved so great that he euthanized the dog.

Human Stewardship and Dog Welfare

Another characteristic feature of Polish dog memoirs is their strong humanitarian message. All the books analyzed in this chapter address the problem of dog welfare and appeal to a sense of duty and responsibility in our relations with companion animals. Similar issues are rarely discussed in contemporary American dog books. Perhaps the American audience no longer needs to be reminded that companion animals enjoy certain rights which have to be respected. However, in Poland, where many village dogs are still chained and some urban dogs get abandoned when they do not fit the holiday plans, the need to educate and propagate fair treatment of animals remains urgent. Dorota Sumińska's policy of adopting old, crippled, unwanted dogs "to convince them that life among humans does not have to be bad" stems from both compassion and a sense of guilt (Sumińska, 2008, p. 314). The author wants to make up for the wrongs these creatures have experienced from other people. Surprisingly, in her appeal for the fair treatment of animals Sumińska does not refer directly to the ideas propagated by the animal rights discourse, perhaps assuming these arguments would sound too radical to the wide Polish audience. Instead, she appeals to the ethic of kindness for all living creatures evoking a traditional, Christian sense of stewardship for animals seen as God's gift to test our charity and morality (Sumińska, 2008, p. 319).

The metaphor of a happy extended family in which both humans and animals can live in joy, peace, and harmony propagated by Sumińska in her memoir is very much indebted to the ideas first spread by 19th-century moralists and educators in Britain and America. According to Grier (2006), "kindness to animals was one part of an expanded sense of stewardship for dependent others who could not survive in the world without special attention and care" (p. 130). It was universally believed that to grow up as respectable middle-class citizens children must learn how to love and take proper care of domestic animals. Tender loving care directed toward an animal with no economic value "demonstrated that a home was functioning as it ought to" (Mason, 2005, p. 13). We find a similar reasoning in Sumińska's rationale behind the adoption of old, abandoned, or terminally ill dogs. In the last chapter of her autobiography, titled "The Way to Live," the author explains that, in her opinion, true moral worth is best estimated by a person's love and willingness to serve others, humans and animals alike (Sumińska, 2008, p. 333).

Death of the Dog

Traditionally, the motif of the dog's death has been used in literature and art as a painful reminder of human transience and mortality. Such conventional treatment of the motif can be found, for example, in renowned poet and writer Jarosław Iwaszkiewicz's *Diaries,* written between the 1960s and 1980s. Acknowledging a connection between the death of his favorite dog and his own demise, Iwaszkiewicz (2011) confesses:

> Tropek's death was for me something terrible and unexpected. This shows how old I am; the event others would consider a trifle became a grave experience for me and I am quite sure that it shortened my own life a few years. To make things worse, I began to imagine that Tropek is waiting for me just around the corner of eternity and that he will be so happy about my arrival. (p. 470)

The pages of Iwaszkiewicz's diary in his last years of life are permeated with a sense of loss. Among recollections of departed relatives and friends, reports from funerals, and notes about his own failing health, the grieving writer returns again and again to the loss of a beloved dog (pp. 472–473, 475, 477, 479, 501). Mourning the dead companion, he at the same time grieves for himself, now deprived of a "last true friend" (p. 471) and a "loving heart" (p. 501).

On the one hand, Iwaszkiewicz's (2011) musings on the dog's "unconditional love" as superior to feeble human affections seem rather naïve and sentimental: "I have failed him and I could not explain anything to him because he was only 'a mere animal'" (p. 501). On the other hand, the dogs in the *Diaries*—both those left at home and those met during travels—attract the elderly writer's attention as creatures so close to humans in pain and death. In one passage Iwaszkiewicz recollects an old, stray bitch, emaciated and bleeding from the mouth, on the hotel street in Taormina, Sicily. The scent of blood provokes a young, well-groomed dog on a leash to attack her. Though the bitch manages to escape, the peaceful, elegant street has suddenly lost its whole charm. Moved by the scene, Iwaszkiewicz asks rhetorically: "What is all the splendor of Taormina to this bitch? Why does she have to suffer? What is suffering?" and answers with resignation that animal suffering seems to him especially "horrible" and "senseless" (p. 386). Faced with animal misery or torment the writer struggles with a sense of guilt toward his own dog because he was absent from home at the hour of his dog's death. Unable to say goodbye to his dying friend, Iwaszkiewicz is now haunted by the dog's ghostly presence, half fearing, half expecting to see him any time among the shadows of those who went away (p. 505).

The analogy between animal and human death is also explored by Andrzej Stasiuk (2012) in "Suka" (The bitch), a short nonfiction story about an old family bitch. While all the stories included in the *Grochów*[12] collection are linked by the theme of death and dying, Stasiuk's decision to ponder the meaning of animal death alongside the death of close friends and relatives should be read, I believe, as a subtle undermining of dominant cultural paradigms. The death of an animal has never been considered as equal to human death, which is also reflected in Polish language.[13] The bitch—her name is never given, as if she were an emblem of any old family dog—lies dying on the porch. She has lost control of her senses: hearing, sight, and smell. She can hardly move or go outside to relieve herself so her sleeping rug is soiled and needs to be changed frequently. As the writer frankly admits, this old, infirm, smelly body irritates him sometimes:

> I pass her by dozens of times, go over her emaciated body and there are moments when I feel impatient. As if her life and my warm

> feelings were ebbing away at the same time. I bend down to pet her. What was once a natural gesture has now become deliberate. (Stasiuk, 2012, p. 35)

The bitch is no longer useful—she will neither bark a warning nor wag a tail to greet a man returning home. As her guardian, Stasiuk is fascinated and simultaneously appalled by the fact that he has witnessed this dog's whole life, a process whereby a living creature has been slowly turning into a dying body. It is his old bitch—immobile, useless, weak, and dependent on others—that makes him consider the prevailing paradoxical attitude toward death at the beginning of the 21st century. We wish to protect and prolong human life—Stasiuk writes—but we are unprepared to face "useless life." The old, the disabled, and the terminally ill have been removed from the sight of the living to end their lives hidden in hospitals and nursing homes. Old, dying animals can also be removed or "put to sleep" when they have become useless.

Hesitant, Stasiuk considers the ethical meaning of such an act:

> She sleeps all the time. In fact, nothing would happen if we made the injection. She would simply go on sleeping. She would no longer soil herself nor fall down. She would stop dragging her back paws or eating her own feces. She would no longer suffer and it would be a relief for us too, because it is not easy to look at somebody (is a dog a "somebody"?) eating her own feces. Nothing would happen. (Stasiuk, 2012, p. 40)

Eventually, the writer's decision not to interfere with time or fate is neither dictated by emotions nor a post-humanistic belief that a dog resembles a person and has a right to die of natural causes. There are no tears, no sentimental recollections of the dog's love, no sense of gratitude for the services rendered to humans. Instead, Stasiuk evokes humanistic respect for "useless life," whether human or animal, fearing that euthanasia—for the time being limited to animals—will sooner or later become a universally accepted procedure to end human life. In the last moving scene a young cat joins the old bitch in her kennel to sleep in the warmth of her dying body. Apparently, the writer suggests, the old bitch is still useful, if not to humans then to the young cat who seeks her company.

In many American narratives of shared life, the death of a dog has a symbolic value because a dog's demise eventually leads to a spiritual rebirth of the dog's guardian. These are, for the most part, "books about death—how to anticipate it, how to participate in it, how to survive it.... Death is all but inescapable, if only to mark a space for closure, both to the intensity of the relationship between guardian and dog as well as to the emotional life of the guardian, who must learn to grieve" (Caesar, 2009, p. 58). For this reason, American authors usually ponder in conclusion on how their life has changed because of a relationship with a special dog. Dean Koontz's tribute to his angelic Golden Retriever Trixie in *Big Little Life* is quite typical in this respect. The grieving author is convinced that Trixie has restored "his sense of wonder," inspired him to take up new subjects in his writing, made him less cynical and more loving as a person (Koontz, 2011, pp. 112–114, 141). Dogs teach humans how to love, how to enjoy life and even make them feel closer to God. All in all, it is no longer enough for the American dog to be a man's (or a woman's) best friend: now "they are expected to be man's saviors" (Caesar, 2009, p. 56).

For all the emotional havoc it may cause, a dog's death in Polish memoirs does not lead to any radical changes in the guardian's lifestyle or a professed system of values. Dorota Sumińska's grief over Wiwa—a beloved companion of her childhood—was intense but brief. Like many American authors who treat the dog as an extension of the self, she perceived the bitch as her animal alter ego and felt as if a part of her had passed away: "I cannot explain it in a rational way. Wiwa was not only my love. She was also me, in a way. I believe that there are people who can understand what I mean" (Sumińska, 2008, p. 171). Though she has paid tribute to Wiwa in all of her books and felt deeply grateful for the love and care given by the bitch to a little lonely girl, she has never considered the dog her savior. In *Who Is Barking?* Ewa Szulc chooses to remain silent about the details of Sabra's and Rafek's deaths—a decision totally at odds with the current practice of American authors who agonize over their dog's painful and protracted dying and their own sense of abandonment.[14] An essential function of such grief narratives is to "countervail depressive muteness and avenge against the passivity one experiences in the face of death. Writing here serves both as a testimony to the dog's life and as a gift to the departed.... But it also insists on sharing the testimony of loss with others in a bid to reverse the social foreclosure of grief" (Kuzniar, 2006, p. 144).

Bogumiła Śpiewakowska's *Teraz jestem w Tęczowym Moście* (I am at the Rainbow Bridge now) is—as far as I know—the only Polish grief narrative. In fact, Śpiewakowska's decision to write a memoir about her devastating sense of loss after her dog's death can be read as an act of defiance against established Polish cultural norms, which still consider mourning a pet problematic and perhaps disturbing. Not finding anything that could be of assistance in her native culture, the author resorts to a foreign cultural concept—the Rainbow Bridge—a vision of heaven where pets and guardians can be together. It gives her hope that "all is not lost, nothing has ended, a fresh start is possible, not now, not just yet, perhaps in many years, in another life" (Śpiewakowska, 2009, p. 184).

The book is divided into two parts. In the first part the author recounts with nostalgia happy years spent with Floksia—a mutt bitch found in a community garden, while in the second part Floksia narrates the same story from her own perspective. The dog is imagined as speaking from the Rainbow Bridge, ensuring the bereft guardian of her love and awaiting their final reunion. Though the belief that animals have souls and can accompany human souls to heaven is at least as old as a Christian legend of Saint Roch (1295–1327), who pleaded for his dog to enter Paradise, its modern version goes a step further, suggesting that all loved companion animals, not just a select few, will accompany their guardians to heaven. *I Am at the Rainbow Bridge Now* clearly manifests the worldwide appeal of the concept of the Rainbow Bridge to dog guardians.

Dog as a Guardian's "Savior" in Fiction

Interestingly, the motif of the dog as a savior, so common in American memoirs and absent from Polish life narratives, has been successfully employed in two recent chick lit novels: *Niosąca radość* (One who brings joy) by Krzysztof Czarnota (2003) and *Dopóki pies nas nie rozłączy* (Till dog do us part) by Romuald Pawlak (2011). Czarnota's novel tells the story of Wojtek, a successful, handsome yuppie whose life suddenly takes on a different course the day he runs over a homeless dog and then, feeling remorseful, takes the dying animal to a vet. The bitch's life is saved by a young, lovely vet, and while the dog, a black Berger de Brie, slowly recuperates, Wojtek feels attracted to both the animal and her attractive doctor—Marysia. After he has eventually decided to adopt the bitch, his lonely life begins to change. Much to his surprise, Wojtek discovers that taking care of the convalescent dog gives him plenty of satisfaction as for the first time in his adult life he feels responsible for the welfare of another being.

Moreover, Pointa, as he has named the dog, changes his daily routine as he spends more time outdoors, takes up jogging and karate, and finally gives up smoking. The dog's joy of life seems infectious, and in her company Wojtek feels calm, relaxed, and simply happy. Soon, he falls in love with Marysia and, under her guidance, starts horseback riding lessons. A new hobby soon turns into a real passion that allows him to stay close to nature and enjoy contact with animals. Eventually, Wojtek leaves behind his hectic life in the big city, buys a large piece of land, and makes plans to breed horses. Taking stock of his new life he feels deeply satisfied, and though he himself considers Marysia a *spiritus movens* of this revolutionary change, Marysia attributes "the miracle" to Pointa's influence: "Everything you have mentioned happened not because of me but because of this poor, stray dog who got under the wheels of your car. If it weren't for Pointa, we would have never met and you would probably still live your old life" (Czarnota, 2003, p. 145).

As in many American dog memoirs, the dog's unexpected death at the end of the novel marks the beginning of a new stage in her guardian's life. Pointa dies suddenly of some unspecified infection, leaving Wojtek crushed with grief:

> I cried as if my closest friend has died. Even today, when I recollect this time, I am moved to tears. I have never really accepted this loss and probably I never will. Some will say that I am being melodramatic. A dog is just a dog. Only someone who does not love animals can say something like that. In a strange, unexplained way

> I feel her presence all the time. I cannot explain this but I feel that she is still close by, that she looks after me. (Czarnota, 2003, p. 152)

Pointa is represented as a truly exceptional dog in the novel—she is the One Who Brings Joy, as her metaphorical name indicates. Moreover, her accidental appearance and her unusual intelligence combined with her positive influence on the narrator fit perfectly the formula of the dog as an angel in disguise or "a potential bearer of 'otherworldly wisdom'" common to American dog books (Caesar, 2009, p. 57). Although her sudden death spoils—at least to some extent—the happy ending, it makes perfect sense if we consider the book as a fictional equivalent of a dog memoir. If Pointa's mission is to show the meaning of life to a shallow, materialistic yuppie, then once he has found true love and a worthy aim in life, she can safely leave him to his own devices, watching over him from afar. Marysia is not only convinced of the dog's providential role in Wojtek's life, but she also believes Pointa has a soul that may be reborn into a human body in her next incarnation.[15] In short, the novel implies that a dog is not "just a dog" but a spiritual being destined to cheer, help, and guide his or her human guardians whenever they need it.

A less realistic treatment of a savior-dog motif is to be found in Romuald Pawlak's *Till Dog Do Us Part.* In the opening scene the Lord of Creation appears in person to speak to a three-month-old puppy and ask for his help. Soon, by God's decree, Platon, a black Miniature Poodle, is sent to repair a failing relationship between Michał and Renia. The young woman, who is afraid that Michał wants to leave her, buys a dog hoping that the animal will function as a baby would, creating a net of shared obligations and responsibilities. As can be predicted, Michał, afraid of any new commitments, protests at first against buying a dog, any dog, but especially a purebred Poodle because to him all Poodles are "mean, spiteful and stupid" (Pawlak, 2011, p. 10). Although Egon is initially a bone of contention between the couple, Michał's determination to not get involved in "the dog business" soon fades. He begins to enjoy walking the dog and teaching him new tricks. When, despite his miniature size, Egon bravely attacks a burglar and defends his family, Michał comes to appreciate the dog's character. One night, when the couple is happily reunited, the Lord of Creation reappears to thank the dog for what he has done and suggests he can retire now: "You can run away from them or I will take your soul, and the body will die and you will be born again" (Pawlak 2011, p. 282). Egon politely declines as he sees a new task ahead—Michał's boss definitely needs his help.

Though Pawlak clearly resorts to a conventional dog-savior motif in the book, he simultaneously subverts it for comic effect. The dog's appearance in Michał and Renia's life is not accidental but has been carefully planned by God Himself. The idea that the Lord of Creation chooses a mischievous Miniature Poodle to act as his four-footed angel in disguise seems genuinely funny. Moreover, in the world represented in the book, a "mere" dog can easily communicate with God, while humans—seemingly "superior" to animals in their spirituality—remain strangely unaware of any metaphysical dimensions of their existence. Having saved his guardians, the dog refuses to depart from this world, thus breaking with convention again. While the couple is to begin a new life as Michał has finally agreed to marry Renia, the new life looks suspiciously similar to the old one, plus the dog. All in all, it turns out that Egon's mission was not so much to change Michał's future in any radical way but to make him appreciate the status quo: Renia's love and their stable, if not very passionate, relationship.

Unlike Czarnota, who treats human-canine relations with utmost seriousness, Pawlak presents some aspects of contemporary pet-keeping and dog breeding in Poland in a satirical light. For example, as a novice in the world of pet owners, Michał pokes fun at the new, fashionable methods of socializing the dog his fiancée wishes to implement. According to the article on behavioral psychology she has read online, the guardian should scold the object itself rather than the dog chewing on it. Unconvinced, Michał decides to give it a try: "When Egon started to chew on the fridge cord, I bellowed: bad cord, very bad, very, very bad cord!!!" Alarmed at the noise, Michał's elderly neighbor comes to intervene and advises him to put some lemon juice on the cord. "So much for behavioral psychology," Michał comments ironically (Pawlak, 2011, pp. 47–48). The narrator is also critical of dog shows which, in his opinion, are driven solely by human, not animal, concerns and needs. The sight of helpless, stressed out champions in cramped cages, sprayed with cosmetics and put on display, makes him angry enough "to howl like a wolf and to drive away all this company"

(Pawlak, 2011, p. 14). Seeing his negative reaction, Renia promises not to enter their dog in a show, though actually she plans otherwise.

As the plot unfolds, Michał secretly teaches Egon some tricks to ruin his chances at the dog show, yet when the big day comes his loyalty to Renia wins. Though he eventually does nothing to spoil Egon's chances at the show, he has some mixed feelings about the dog's participation in it:

> He was a happy dog, certainly not a slave. But as a medalist he has now became a part of the system: dogs in cages, all this horrible grooming, masking of deficiencies as if the thickness of the coat was more important than whether a dog likes children or wants to attack them. (Pawlak, 2011, p. 274)

Michał's dilemma stems from the fact that he thinks about dogs as companion animals, rather than commodities, and turning a man's best friend into an object of wheeling and dealing seems unethical to him. For Michał, the biggest problem with dog shows is that they satisfy human, not animal, desires for social recognition, prestige, and high status. As he rhetorically asks: "Who were the medals, certificates and written assessments for? The dog would have preferred a piece of sausage though nobody was going to give it to him here" (Pawlak, 2011, p. 8). Egon himself remains silent on the matter of dog shows and any other problematic issues in human-canine relations, though parts of the book are narrated from his point of view. Neither does he ever criticize his guardians. Such restraint seems surprising in light of the fact that literary dogs have been conventionally employed to attack the anthropocentric view of the world and instrumental treatment of animals.

The World According to a Pet

In Western literary tradition, the satirical motif of a philosophical or "cynical" dog, who suddenly finds himself able to speak and thus can comment critically on human affairs, first appeared in *Dialogues of the Dead* from an ancient satirist, Lucian of Samosata, to be revived in the Renaissance by Bonaventure des Periers in his allegorical work *Cymbalum Mundi* (1537)

(Ziolkowski, 1983, pp. 97–99). In Cervantes's *Colloquy of the Dogs* (1613), two "learned" dogs—Scipio and Berganza—narrate their picaresque adventures in sophisticated language. Less philosophically minded but no less entertaining were the dog narrators in "it-narratives" or "novels of circulation," a genre that reached its peak popularity in 18th century Great Britain (Rutkowska, 2014, pp. 463–470). These satirical works were based on a premise that common material objects such as money, articles of clothing, or furniture, as well as animals, could narrate the incidents of their lives and observe and comment on the actions and characters of their human owners. Last but not least, "talking dogs" figured as heroes in sentimental animal autobiographies such as *Beautiful Joe* (1893) by M. M. Saunders, which advocated humanitarian treatment of domestic animals in the late 19th century. For all their differences, the genres that have relied on an animal's point of view have traditionally employed it as an effective defamiliarizing device capable of strengthening the satirical or didactic potential of the text. It has to be noted, however, that neither of these literary traditions has influenced Polish literature in any significant manner, which probably explains why dog narrators have appeared in Polish fiction for adult readers only since the beginning of the 21st century.

As a nonhuman member of the household, intelligent and sentient yet silent, the dog is at the same time inside and outside the human world, a position which enables him to provide a critical assessment of human ways and an explanation of his dog ways for the readers' sake. Bolek, an elderly Dachshund who acts as a narrator in Dorota Sumińska's (2010) novel *Świat według psa* (The world according to a dog), fulfills both of these roles yet he is, first and foremost, a pet, deprived of agency and dependent on human whims. Like his 18th- and 19th-century predecessors in it-narratives and sentimental novels, Bolek changes hands and meets various people along the way, some good and caring, others indifferent or hostile. His first guardian enjoys Bolek's company but is often away from home, while his wife considers the dog's presence a nuisance. When the baby is born, the woman, identified by the narrator only as "a human bitch" (the pun is intended), insists on getting rid of the dog. Embittered, Bolek comments: "People treat us like an armchair or a meat grinder. They give us away, or lend, or give to someone for a time" (Sumińska, 2010, p. 19). Lucky for Bolek, his new guardian, Irma, a gentle, elderly lady with a big heart, never treats animals as objects. As she explains: "The dog can give you so much love. It is a priceless treasure; both the love and the dog" (Sumińska, 2010, p. 46).

In Irma's house a dog and a cat function as cherished companions rather than pets, and their needs, both physical and emotional, are given due respect. Irma, who often feels lonely, enjoys talking to Bolek. The dog, for his part, is happy to become her silent confidant, though at times he feels frustrated by his inability to comfort her with words. "Don't look at me like that, don't look at me like that—easier said than done. What else can a dog do, even the most intelligent? He can only look with understanding, look with sympathy and love" (Sumińska, 2010, p. 42). Contrasted with indifference at best and callousness or even deliberate cruelty at worst, Irma's attitude toward animals seems truly exceptional. In her last will and testament she makes sure that Bolek and the other animals will be provided for and will stay at her house until the end of their days.

Trying to describe "the world according to the dog," or rather the world according to a pet, Sumińska resorts to her own experience as a dog guardian, the expert knowledge of a veterinarian, amateur behavioral psychology and, occasionally, animal rights discourse. Acting as the author's mouthpiece, Bolek criticizes instrumental treatment of pets. Human demands of "absolute obedience" are simply unrealistic. Why is a dog, a sentient and emotional creature, expected to act as if he were a machine that can be turned off when a guardian leaves home? (Sumińska, 2010, p. 43). Some common assumptions about dogs' favorite activities reveal human ignorance. Going for a walk, Bolek explains, is much more than going to the toilet. For dogs, the experience is in fact comparable to visiting the library or the post office, participating in a social gathering, or looking for a prospective mate (Sumińska 2010, p. 45). As for the art of sniffing, it can disclose secrets humans will never know. The nose tells Bolek, for example, that the baby born to his first guardian has not been fathered by him, and he discovers the boy is ill before the doctors have diagnosed him. The dog is able to smell a new life in a woman's womb and to feel approaching death.

Though hard evidence of dogs' extrasensory perception hardly exists, the idea that dogs can see ghosts or detect invisible presences is widespread in popular culture. In her novel, Sumińska also resorts to this common motif to introduce the ghost of Władek, Irma's long-deceased husband. Władek explains to Bolek that the human-canine bond has also its metaphysical dimension because when a dog dies, a human guardian spirit appears to lead his soul safely to the afterlife. Not only dogs enjoy this special bond with humans, but every living creature "shares its soul with a human being. Otherwise, neither mine nor yours would be complete" (Sumińska, 2010, p. 74).

Both in the novel and in her autobiography, Sumińska tackles a fundamental question, "Do animals have souls?," and answers it in the affirmative, contradicting the official Catholic teaching, which denies animal spirituality and sees no place for them in heaven. While in fiction she resorts to the idea of the interconnectedness of all living souls, in her memoir she evokes the arguments of Jean Prieur, who wrote that "the animal is a soul: *animal est anima*" (quoted in Sumińska, 2008, p. 330). If animals have souls and are indeed our "lesser brothers," then their inhuman treatment may be considered a sin. That is why one of the characters in the novel feels compelled to confess at his deathbed that he had killed the dog, thus extending the commandment "Thou shall not kill" to include animals, even though such interpretation was always considered faulty by Church Fathers. The novel ends with a car crash; afterward Bolek finds himself healthy again, running with young Irma and Władek in a sunny meadow. Władek tells him that now they will now all live together "in a new home" (Sumińska, 2010, p. 250). The vision of heaven in the closing scene of the novel resembles the Rainbow Bridge, testifying that this concept, so common now in the Anglo-American culture, is growing in popularity in Poland.

Kindred Spirits

Unlike Bolek, Wabi, the dog narrator in Marek Stokowski's (2014) *Kino krótkich filmów* (Short films movie theater), does not consider himself a subordinated pet but a "friend" to his guardian, M. The yellow mutt strikes the reader as a reliable and self-assured narrator, an ordinary dog who happens to accompany an extraordinary man: hypersensitive, empathic, and spiritual. M., a man in his 30s who had remained in a coma for 20 years, now, after a miraculous recovery, tries to build a new life working as a self-appointed "tree tuner" in the forests of northern Poland. While some people consider M. a freak or suspect he is simply crazy because he hears the music of trees, Wabi wholeheartedly believes in his friend's insight into metaphysical reality (Stokowski, 2014, p. 229).

Wabi's role is that of a kindred spirit or "a faithful shadow, a companion who keeps at a distance, an unobtrusive guardian" (Stokowski, 2014, p. 11). Indeed, there are some secrets M. can confide only in the dog as even his landlady, in spite of being a generous and charitable woman, would not understand him. There are also some services that can be rendered only by the dog, always close by and on alert when daydreaming M. loses contact with reality and starts talking with the angelic beings he got to know while he was comatose. As a True Keeper, Wabi brings his man back to earth by simply pulling at his trouser leg. When, in the middle of winter, M. decides to walk to Sweden to visit the woman he loves, the dog accompanies him, helping on the road whenever human methods fail. Wabi's skillful negotiations with a German Shepherd guarding the passage through the river gets them to the other side, his ability to read body language gets them both a free meal at a building site, and his sense of smell allows them to find their way when lost. What is even more important is that Wabi takes the lead whenever M. wants to give up his quest. In the culminating scene of the novel, the dog leads the man back to the beach, where, miraculously, they find the Baltic Sea frozen. The book ends with the image of the man and the dog walking together on ice toward Sweden in the falling snow.

Though he modestly characterizes himself as "an ordinary village mutt, not any intelligent professor," Wabi is indeed well versed in human psychology and understands M. better than any human friend would (Stokowski, 2014, p. 19). From the dog's perspective, M.'s behavior is no more bizarre than that of other people, and Wabi's reliable narrative lends credibility to the most unexpected decisions or actions of his guardian. Interestingly, it is the dog who speaks for the man—silent, bewildered, or lost in thoughts—explaining his emotional reactions to the readers, not the other way around. In Stokowski's novel, Wabi functions much in the same way as Mr. Bones does in Paul Auster's (1999) *Timbuktu*. In both books the dogs become devoted, loyal friends and confidantes of male outsiders who do not fit in with society and find it difficult to confide in other people. The human-canine bond as represented by Auster and Stokowski is based on interspecies trust, responsibility, and camaraderie. Both Mr. Bones and Wabi are playing the role of down-to-earth Sancho Panzas to their dreamy Don Quixotes. They not only accompany their guardians in the wanderings but also speak on their behalf because "the dogs can be articulate, especially when they have to speak for the man who does not want to or cannot say anything but it would be good if somebody knew that he is alive, that he exists" (Stokowski, 2014, p. 10). Even though the figure of a dog narrator has been conventionally employed in literary works for satirical purposes, Wabi's view of humanity is neither harsh nor condescending. In general, he is of the opinion that "people overestimate their role. Without them the world would go round as well" (Stokowski, 2014, p. 51). But like his guardian, Wabi believes there is some goodness in all the people they encounter on the road—only some of them need proper "tuning," just like the trees M. heals.

One of the central themes in Stokowski's novel is the belief in the power of storytelling. Apart from tuning trees, M. collects stories in the woods. He believes that these short narratives, filled with magical realism or absurd humor, may connect people who listen to them, heal their wounds, move them to action, or offer an imaginative escape from mundane reality. Intrigued by this idea and willing to help in disseminating "therapeutic" stories, Wabi willingly takes upon himself the role of the helper:

> I have M's consent. As a dog I remember all the words faithfully and I can share them with you. Attention, everyone! To all those not checked by *Homo sapiens* speciesist superiority, those who like us—*Canis lupus familiaris*—enjoy playing with a stick or a ball, those who can do without looking serious and grandiose, I suggest a show of short movies or, to put it differently, a few minutes of silly fun. I will throw stories. Fetch! (Stokowski, 2014, p. 20)

Using a metaphor based on his experiences as a dog, Wabi suggests "throwing" stories at the readers much as a man would throw a stick or a ball to a dog. Though both actions seem ordinary and simple, "a few minutes of silly fun" are in fact essential for the well-being of dogs and humans alike.

Beware of the (Too Human) Dog

In contrast to Wabi, Albrecht, the narrator of Izabella Szolc's (2011) murder mystery *Strzeż się psa* (Beware of the dog), is stereotypically patronizing and acerbic as regards humans. Albrecht, a purebred Bloodhound, is a big-headed, philosophic erudite and, apparently, the first Polish dog detective. Because he grew up in a family of academics specializing in the art and culture of the Italian Renaissance, he is well versed in European history, philosophy, and literature. His command of both Italian and Latin is likewise impressive. Albrecht's story takes the form of a neurotic monologue peppered with numerous references to the classics on the one hand and allusions to popular culture on the other. Obviously, such authorial choice of a narrative persona determines the satirical, even sarcastic, tone of the book in which the social worlds of urban dogs and their yuppie guardians are compared, contrasted, and critically assessed.

Since Szolc clearly resorts to the literary tradition of "learned dogs" in her book, she represents the dogs as intelligent, articulate, and more world-wise than their human guardians. Although Sumińska's and Stokowski's dog narrators are portrayed in an anthropomorphic way, the authors try to preserve at least some plausibility, referring, for example, to the dogs' unique sense of smell, pack dynamics, and instinctive behavior. In contrast to Bolek or Wabi, who occasionally remind the readers that they are dogs, Albrecht always reasons, feels, and reacts as if he were a man. There are, for instance, some obvious erotic undertones in the way Albrecht describes his love for the attractive female guardian:

> Laura came to bed. I was waiting for her. I felt quite ill. This illness had even its Latin name: *morbus amor*. Characteristic, recurrent

> symptoms: your throat tightens, your heart is racing, you begin to salivate (instead of sweating like other species), your muscles quiver … (Szolc, 2011, p. 15)

When Laura snaps at the dog for taking the pillow, he comments: "Aren't these like pillow talks of long-married happy couples?" He is jealous of her boyfriends and refers to each of them, condescendingly as "her current dick" (Szolc, 2011, p. 15). To complicate matters further, Albrecht suffers not only because of the species barrier that separates him from Laura but also from a castration complex. Laura's mother had him neutered and while in the company of other dogs he tries to compensate for the loss of "masculinity" with his wit and erudition, he can neither forget nor accept his sexual deficiency, thinking obsessively about sex, both human and canine, and pining both for Laura as well as an attractive neighbor—a Saluki bitch.

Anthropomorphization reaches its peak in the scenes of Albrecht's investigation of dog murders. Contrary to the readers' expectations, Albrecht hardly ever resorts to his superb sense of smell while gathering evidence or tracking the murderer. Thus, instead of "sniffing around," Albrecht interrogates domestic animals much as any human detective would. Eventually, the murderer is not identified by his scent (even though he is the man Laura works for so Albrecht should immediately recognize it) but thanks to information provided by Albrecht's secret informer—a local cat. A weak plot and extreme anthropomorphization of the dog sleuth may be one of the reasons *Beware of the Dog* fails as an engaging murder mystery. All the pleasure the readers may have derived from imagining how an actual dog would have gone about finding a murderer is lost as Albrecht's methods are in no way unconventional or even doglike. The dog's reasoning is simply too human to surprise or impress the readers as an example of an animal mind at work. Though the blurb advertises the book as "a tribute to dog's intelligence," it can hardly be read as such because canine intelligence is imagined as no different from human. Dogs represented in the work mirror humans in the way they perceive, organize, and act in the world.

There is, for instance, a clear social stratification in the canine community, with urban, purebred dogs functioning as the elite and strays as the underdogs. The breed and social position of a dog's guardian determine the animal's fate: some pets are acquired and abandoned at a whim; others—especially fashionable purebreds—have been bought to confirm their guardians' social status and to profit from puppies; still others, usually mutts or country dogs, function as human slaves and watchdogs. The author also makes use of a conventional theme of class tension between the poor dogs who envy the rich ones their privileges and comforts and the rich dogs who are afraid and suspicious of mutts or strays. Unsurprisingly, a former stray dog with a mysterious past turns out to be a canine renegade who helps to lure innocent victims into the woods to be murdered. Tramp—the villain dog—has been corrupted by Pryza, an unscrupulous newly rich businessman who plans to capitalize on the human-canine bond by building what Albrecht ironically calls a "NecroDonald." It is to be a commercial complex including a dog cemetery, a shelter (just in case a bereft guardian wants a replacement pet), and a restaurant for those visiting the cemetery. In order to convince the local community to agree to his plans Pryza needs dead dogs, hence the murders. For all its improbability, the book's plot is based on a sound observation: In contemporary Polish society dog owners constitute an important segment of the market; therefore, echoing their sentiments and catering to their needs may be a good, if not always ethical, business strategy.

Thus, it is possible to read Szolc's book not only as a (failed) detective story but as a voice in the current debate on human-animal relations. It is noteworthy that the author, who is herself an animal rights activist, has offered her royalties from *Beware of the Dog* to Viva!, a Polish-based non-governmental organization that raises funds to run a number of campaigns to protect domestic animals—especially horses and dogs—from cruelty, neglect, and death. In her novel, Szolc satirizes those dog-keeping practices she finds objectionable, while the last pages of her book contain information about Viva!'s campaigns. Perhaps the author's decision to anthropomorphize domestic animals in such an exaggerated manner was dictated by her desire to show them as quasi-persons, whose intelligence, sensibility, and emotionality demand to be respected much in the same way as human needs and rights are respected.

Conclusion

Dog memoirs and dog novels are a recent phenomenon in Polish literature as the earliest "dog books" addressed to adult readers were published in the last decades of the 20th century. This late start can be explained, primarily, by the historical factors which influenced attitudes toward domestic animals, including dogs, and their literary representations in Poland over the last 150 years. First of all, it needs to be remembered that the practice of pet-keeping was closely connected with the rise of the middle-class in Western Europe (Thomas, 1983, pp. 117–120). This process was hampered in 19th-century Poland by the lack of political sovereignty and economic dependence on partitioning powers: Russia and Prussia. The dogs of the Polish nobility did not function in the same way as middle-class pets in Victorian households. The hounds were valued as hunting companions but rarely perceived as "best friends" or family members in Polish manor houses. As a result, the relationship with them was not as intimate as the bond with horses, traditionally considered the most intelligent and noble among the domestic animals. Numerous poems, stories, anecdotes, and portraits exist about exceptional horses in 19th-century Polish Romantic culture, but dogs are mentioned almost exclusively in the context of their usefulness in hunting.

Moreover, for a long time the Polish educated elite—less numerous than the British or American middle-class—had more pressing concerns than the protection of domestic animals against cruelty. The question of animal rights was secondary to the question of national independence in 19th-century Poland. Even though the first Polish society for the protection of animals was founded in Warsaw as early as 1864, it operated only locally and its influence on the public opinion was rather limited. Concern for animal welfare did not become a topic of public debate until the 1980s, and it was only at that time that the ideas propagated by animal rights activists from Western European countries produced some lasting response in Poland.

However, in the last few decades a number of factors have contributed to making dogs an attractive subject for popular culture and academic research alike. The growing importance of companion animals in Western urban societies has been noted by sociologists and psychologists since the 1970s, and Poland is no exception to the rule. As family ties weaken, the dogs rise in status, being treated less as subordinated, subservient pets and more as surrogate children or substitutes for absent human family members. New medical, sociological, and anthropological research into human-canine interdependence, and the emergence of animal studies, have increased human interest in or fascination with dogs.

Generally, current representations of dogs in Polish memoirs and novels are indebted to Anglo-American cultural products, especially sentimental and largely anthropomorphic literary and cinematic depictions of dogs either as charming pets or steadfast companions. Yet for all the similarities in plots and motifs, Polish and American dog books differ considerably. The most crucial difference is the role attributed to the dog in the human life story. In American dog memoirs, the dog invariably acts as a "savior" to his guardian, changing the course of his life, improving his family relations, and even influencing his professional career. In Polish life narratives it is most frequently a man who saves a dog (not the other way around) and then devotes time, energy, and money to make the dog healthy and happy again. Another distinguishing characteristic lies in the presentation of family life since Polish authors rarely focus on one-on-one relationships. There are other animals in the house, as well as a human partner who shares the guardian's passion for dogs and helps with the duties. Last but not least, Polish books rarely end with the dog's death or function as grief memoirs.

Interestingly, the American dog-savior scenario has been taken over by Polish chick lit fiction. In recent such novels by Czarnota and Pawlak, a dog suddenly appears at a young man's side to alter his life for the better and lead him into psychological maturity. As Alice Kuzniar (2006) notes: "Stories and movies that tell the adventure of a young boy and his dog always involve a socialization process for the boy, often signifying the boy's maturation through the perils the dog encounters" (p. 113). This is also true of the novels in question. Even though the protagonists are young men, they have remained immature in their egotism, selfishness, and lack of concern for others. It is the bond with the dog that opens these male characters to new commitments, makes them realize the value of true love, and helps them find a worthy aim in life. The dogs, it is implied in these books, are not "mere dogs" but rather mysterious spiritual beings, perhaps even tools of divine Providence.

The presence of dog narrators is another recent phenomenon in Polish fiction addressed to adult readers, yet the animal point of view is only occasionally used in these novels for satirical or didactic purposes. In contradistinction to the narrators used in animal sentimental autobiographies such as *Black Beauty* or *Beautiful Joe,* contemporary Polish dog narrators rarely speak *for* animals or their cause. Though they may occasionally reflect on inequalities in human-animal relations, they seem to accept their subordinate status or lack of control over their lives. Strongly humanized or anthropomorphized, Bolek, Wabi, and Albrecht are mainly preoccupied with narrating human adventures and affairs. Bolek and Wabi are cast in the role of kindred spirit, silent confidant, and best friend to the guardian marginalized by the mainstream society (an old woman, a middle-aged "freak"), while Albrecht, more critical than the other two, is represented as a frustrated philosopher. All in all, there is hardly an attempt to imagine these dogs and their thoughts outside the human frame of reference or to render animal consciousness through language or metaphor.

In the light of contemporary animal studies discourse that embraces post-humanism, recent Polish books on the human-canine relationship still belong in the previous era. While American authors alternate between reductive anthropomorphism and puzzling otherness in their portrayals of family dogs, Polish authors feel comfortable only with the former perspective. They rarely acknowledge human-animal kinship or ponder the boundary between the human and animal worlds. They may toy with the idea of giving voice to their "dumb" dogs, but what the dogs "say" confirms rather than questions the anthropocentric paradigm. Moreover, both nonfiction life narratives and novels are based on humanistic conviction that animals are our "lesser brothers" and as such demand human stewardship. The underlying message of many of these books is clear: The measure of our humanity is to treat dogs in a kind and loving way, much as we treat children. Dogs victimized or abandoned by bad guardians deserve to be given a new home and saved from further suffering. Our ethical obligations to them do not stem from the fact that they are persons (for they are not) but rather from the fact that they have been incorporated into our social world. Is this attitude likely to change? Perhaps a short question asked by Stasiuk in *The Bitch*—"Is a dog a 'somebody'?"—will be answered in the positive in the Polish dog memoirs and novels yet to be written.

Notes

1. Jan Grabowski, *Reksio i Pucek* [Reksio and Pucek] (Warszawa: Nasza Księgarnia, 1929); *Puc, Bursztyn i Goście* [Puc, Bursztyn and visitors] (Warszawa: Nasza Księgarnia, 1933); Ewa Szelburg-Zarembina, *Najmilsi* [The favorites] (Białystok: Krajowa Agencja Wydawnicza, 1991).
2. Anna Iwaszkiewiczowa, *Nasze zwierzęta* [Our animals] (Warszawa: Czytelnik, 1978).
3. Romuald Pawlak, *Póki pies nas nie rozłączy* [Till dog do us part] (Warszawa: Nasza Księgarnia, 2011); Ola Trzeciecka, *Jamnik z kluskami* [Dachshund with noodles] (Warszawa: Prószyński i S-ka, 2014); Krzysztof Czarnota, *Niosąca radość* [The one who brings joy] (Poznań: Wydawnictwo Zysk i S-ka, 2003).
4. Dorota Sumińska, Świat *według psa* [The world according to a dog] (Kraków: Wydawnictwo Literackie, 2010); Marek Stokowski, *Stroiciel lasu* [The woods tuner] (Warsaw: Oficyna Wydawnicza Multico, 2010); Marek Stokowski, *Kino krótkich filmów* [Short films movie theater] (Bytom: Wydawnictwo Niecałe, 2014); Izabela Szolc, *Strzeż się psa* [Beware of the dog] (Gdańsk: Oficynka, 2011).
5. Galaktyka Publishing House, which specializes in manuals and hobby books, has published the following American dog memoirs in translation: *Merle's Door: Lessons From a Freethinking Dog* (Harcourt, 2007) by Ted Kerasote; *A Dog Year: Twelve Months, Four Dogs, and Me* (Random House, 2003) and A *Good Dog: The Story of Orson, Who Changed My Life* (Random House, 2006) by John Katz; *Amazing Gracie: A Dog's Tale* (Workman, 2000) by Dan Dye and Mark Beckloff; *Come Back, Como: Winning the Heart of a Reluctant Dog* (HarperCollins, 2009) by Steven Winn; *From Baghdad With Love: A Marine, the War, and a Dog Named Lava* (Lyons Press, 2006) by Jay Kopelman and Melinda Roth; and *A Three Dog Life* (Harcourt, 2006) by Abigail Thomas.

6. Virginia Woolf, *Flush: Biografia* (Kraków: Wydawnictwo Znak, 2009); Joe Randolf Ackerley, *Moja Tulipanka* (Warszawa: Wydawnictwo Studio Emka, 2013).
7. See for example: Rhoda Lerman's *In the Company of Newfies: A Shared Life* (Blue Heaven, 1996); Rick Bass's *Colter: The True Story of the Best Dog I Ever Had* (Houghton Mifflin, 2000); Mark Doty's *Dog Years* (2008); Ted Kerasote's *Merle's Door* (2007); Jon Katz's *A Good Dog* (2006); Dean Koontz's *A Big Little Life: A Memoir of a Joyful Dog* (Hyperion, 2009); John Grogan's *Marley and Me: Life and Love With the World's Worst Dog* (HarperCollins, 2005); and Dan Dye and Mark Beckloff's *Amazing Gracie* (2003). This list is by no means complete as new books are published every year.
8. To give just a few examples: Dorota Sumińska shares her house with 20 companion animals, both dogs and cats; Ewa Szulc writes in her memoir about challenges posed by accommodating two Great Danes and a cat in a tiny flat; Jędrzej Fijałkowski owns two dogs and a cat, and Joanna Sędzikowska runs a "foster family" for abandoned Alaskan Malamutes.
9. American memoirs in which family dogs have been allowed to join a pack or to lead a social life "of their own" are quite rare. See for example: Ted Kerasote's *Merle's Door* (2007) and Rhoda Lerman's *In the Company of Newfies* (1996).
10. All titles and quotes in this chapter translated by Małgorzata Rutkowska.
11. In Poland, Dorota Sumińska enjoys the status of a celebrity veterinarian; she is the author of popular dog manuals and used to host TV shows about domestic animals.
12. Grochów is a borough of Warsaw.
13. Traditionally, one would say of an animal that it croaked *(zdechł)* rather than died *(zmarł)*, although the latter is becoming more common with reference to companion animals.
14. As Ackerley's memoir shows, dog guardians in the past used to be much more reserved in this respect. Ackerley recorded Tulip's death in a single sentence which concluded his book: "Whatever blunders I may have committed in my managements of this animal life, she lived on to the great age of sixteen-and-a-half." Ackerley, J. R. (1965). *My dog Tulip* (p. 172). New York, NY: Tower Publications.
15. Interestingly, the rebirth of a dog into a human body is also the story line in

Garth Stein's *The Art of Racing in the Rain* (2008), where Enzo, the dog narrator, dies and is reborn as a small boy bearing the same name.

References

Auster, P. (1999). *Timbuktu*. New York, NY: Henry Holt.

Caesar, T. (2009). *Speaking of animals: Essays on dogs and others*. Leiden, the Netherlands: Brill.

Czarnota, K. (2003). *Niosąca radość* [One who brings joy]. Poznań, Poland: Wydawnictwo Zysk i S-ka.

Doty, M. (2008). *Dog years: A memoir*. London, UK: Jonathan Cape.

Eakin, P. J. (1999). *How our lives become stories: Making selves*. Ithaca, NY: Cornell University Press.

Fijałkowski, J. (2009). *Emil, czyli kiedy szczęśliwe są psy, szczęśliwy jest cały świat*. [Emil, or when the dogs are happy, the whole world is happy]. Poznań, Poland: Zysk i S-ka.

Grier, K. C. (2006). *Pets in America: A history*. Chapel Hill: University of North Carolina Press.

Grogan, J. (2005). *Marley & me: Life and love with the world's worst dog*. New York, NY: Morrow.

Iwaszkiewicz, J. (2011). *Dzienniki 1964–1980* [The diaries 1964–1980]. Warsaw, Poland: Czytelnik.

Katz, J. (2006). *A good dog: The story of Orson, who changed my life*. New York, NY: Villard Books.

Konecki, K. T. (2005). *Ludzie i ich zwierzęta. Interakcjonistyczno—symboliczna analiza społecznego świata właścicieli zwierząt domowych* [People and their animals: A symbolic interactionist analysis of the social world of pet owners]. Warsaw, Poland: Scholar.

Koontz, D. (2011). *A big little life: A memoir of a joyful dog named Trixie*. New York, NY: Bantham Books.

Kuzniar, A. (2006). *Melancholia's dog: Reflections on our animal kinship*. Chicago, IL: University of Chicago Press.

Mason, J. (2005). *Civilized creatures: Urban animals, sentimental culture, and*

American literature, 1850–1900. Baltimore, MD: Johns Hopkins University Press.

Pawlak, R. (2011). *Póki pies nas nie rozłączy* [Till dog do us part]. Warsaw, Poland: Nasza Księgarnia.

Pinsker, S. (2003). The landscape of contemporary American memoir, *Sewanee Review, 111*(2), 311–320.

Rutkowska, M. (2014). Sentience, suffering and sympathy: Animals in British it-narratives, 1780–1830. In G. Bystydzieńska & E. Harris (Eds.), *From Queen Anne to Queen Victoria: Readings in 18th and 19th century British literature and culture* (Vol. 4; pp. 463–470). Warsaw, Poland: Uniwersytet Warszawski, Ośrodek Studiów Brytyjskich.

Sędzikowska, J. (2012). *Psy z piekła rodem* [The hounds from hell]. Warszawa, Poland: Wydawnictwo Nowy Świat.

Śpiewakowska, B. (2009). *Teraz jestem w Tęczowym Moście* [I am at the Rainbow Bridge now]. Poznań, Poland: Zysk i S-ka.

Stasiuk, A. (2012). *Grochów* [Grochów]. Wołowiec, Poland: Wydawnictwo Czarne.

Stokowski, M. (2014). *Kino krótkich filmów* [Short films movie theater]. Bytom, Poland: Wydawnictwo Niecałe.

Sumińska, D. (2008). *Autobiografia na czterech łapach, czyli historia jednej rodziny oraz psów, kotów, krów, koni, jeży, słoni, węży… i ich krewnych* [A four-footed autobiography or a story of one family and its dogs, cats, cows, horses, hedgehogs, elephants, snakes … and their relatives]. Cracow, Poland: Wydawnictwo Literackie.

Sumińska, D. (2010). Świat *według psa* [The world according to a dog]. Cracow, Poland Wydawnictwo Literackie.

Szolc, I. (2011). *Strzeż się psa* [Beware of the dog]. Gdańsk, Poland: Oficynka.

Szulc, E. (1995). *Kto tu szczeka?* [Who is barking?]. Warsaw, Poland: Elew.

Thomas, K. (1983). *Man and the natural world: Changing attitudes in England 1500–1800.* London, UK: Penguin Books.

Ziolkowski, T. (1983). *Varieties of literary thematics.* Princeton, NJ: Princeton University Press.

6

The Future and the Moment of Animal Suffering in Space: Representations of Laika in Polish Contemporary Art

Dorota Łagodzka

An important sociopolitical discussion took place in Poland in late 2014 and early 2015. It concerned an amendment to the Law on the Protection of Animals Used for Scientific or Educational Purposes, adopted by the local Parliament on January 15. Polish regulations were being adjusted to those of the European Union. The change was caused not so much due to a concern for animals themselves or the quality of research but rather to issues surrounding the of trade of goods and licensing. Public demonstrations aiming to prevent the introduction of regulations that would work to the detriment of animals took place in Warsaw in front of the Parliament building. Protesters filed petitions signed by animal rights and animal welfare organizations, artists, researchers, journalists, celebrities, and everyday citizens. The amendment that was eventually passed states that the ethical committees approving animal experimentation must include representatives of humanities and animal rights organizations (see Dziennik Ustaw Rzeczypospolitej Polskiej, 2015).

Although animal testing of beauty products had already been banned in the European Union by the European Commission (2015; the executive body of the EU), other experiments that are justified scientifically are still permissible. Whereas animal testing for cosmetics is often considered in Europe and North America to be unnecessary and ethically unjustified, medical experiments are looked at in quite a different way because they are believed to guarantee the development of cures that benefit people's health and save lives. The scientific use of animals in space research, however, fits a slightly different category. Aeronautical experiments are deeply rooted in an aura of strangeness and mystery associated with discovering the universe and with the dream of finding life on other planets. Experiments conducted in space, either with or without the use of animals, are beyond the experience of a common person and therefore hard to understand. These experiments are largely kept secret, with neither press nor citizens having much (if any) access to them. And when access to information is available, it is not always up to date. As I am writing this chapter in the spring of 2015, the Web page for an article about animals in space that was written for high school students in 2004 and is currently posted on the National Aeronautics and Space Administration's official website was most recently updated in 2009 (NASAexplores, 2004).

NASA reassures its audience that animals chosen to travel in space are ethically and humanely cared for. Laura Lewis, a member of the NASA Ames Institutional Animal Care and Use Committee, claims:

> Regulations for animal research are more intense than for using people in research because people can give consent. Animals can't object, so people need to work on their behalf. Animal housing rules are more extensive than the requirements for human children day care centers. NASA facilities that house animals for research are accredited by an organization that requires proof that animals are cared for in a facility that meets those standards. (NASAexplores, 2004, para. 11)

According to the same article, the United States Department of Agriculture Animal Welfare Act and the Public Health Services Policy Act both "protect research animals and set minimum standards" when it comes to using them for experiments (NASAexplores, 2004, para. 11).

Only a few animal astronauts have gained popularity so far, but Laika (English translation: Barker), a Soviet crossbred canine from the 1950s, is probably the only one widely known; she is also the subject of a substantial number of representations in visual culture, both early on and nowadays. The glorification of Laika did not happen immediately, though; initially her presence onboard, as Olesya Turkina (2014) writes, "was only cursorily mentioned in a list of items … for studying life functions in the conditions of outer space" (p. 82). Laika took part in the science and technology race between the Soviet Union and the United States (and China as well), a race with a pronounced political background. Placing Laika in orbit around the Earth gave the Soviets an opportunity to (at least temporarily) beat the Americans in the race for the conquest of space. Future U.S. president Lyndon Baines Johnson wrote in his diary at the time: "But now somehow in a new way, the sky seemed almost alien. I also remember the profound shock of realizing that it might be possible for another nation to achieve technical superiority over this great country of ours" (D'Antonio, 2005, p. 42).

Experiments in space have been an important element of politics and propaganda since they began. In fact, they serve the same purpose today, long after the fall of the Iron Curtain. This at least can be interpreted from a quotation by NASA Administrator Charles Bolden, found in an article titled *What's Next for NASA?*:

> As a former astronaut and the current NASA Administrator, I'm here to tell you that American leadership in space will continue for at least the next half-century because we have laid the foundation for success—and failure is not an option. (NASA, 2015)

• • •

In the following text I will discuss the representations of Laika (written in Polish as *Łajka* and in Russian as Лайка) as a particular and unique animal in contemporary Polish art. Three subjects of my analysis are (1) Aleksander Malewski's *Łajka* from 2008, found at the Regional Zachęta Contemporary Art Collection in Szczecin; (2) Agata Zbylut's *Łajka* from 2011, in the collection of the National Museum in Szczecin; and (3) Kaja Rata's *Łajka wróć!*

(Laika come back!) from 2014, recently recognized in the Wilhelm von Blandowski memorial competition for the design of a photographic book organized by the gallery of the Museum in Gliwice, although this work goes far beyond using a single medium. I will also discuss (4) a painting from 2003 by Zbigniew Rogalski, *Untitled (Łajka).* Although the painting does not feature an actual image of Laika (or any other dog), her presence is felt because of the inscription of her name in the artwork.

I look at these works through the prism of real astronomic experiments involving animals. Concepts connected with time—the future, the past, and the present moment, as well as duration or continuation—are essential both in the view of the works themselves and in the historical, social, political, and ethical context. Malewski's art presents the moment of Laika's death onboard Sputnik 2, whereas Zbylut's installation shows a situation right before the experiment which, nevertheless, relates to the future fate of the dog. Rata's book connects the historical Laika with contemporary dogs and a dreamlike vision for the future. Rogalski recalls Laika as the heroine of his childhood fascination with Russian astronautics.

This chapter confronts modern Polish artistic visions of Laika with historical facts and some reflections about animal ethics, based on the

Malewski's installation titled *"Łajka"* is in the form of a Sputnik capsule, modeled on the one that became the dog's coffin. (Artur Malewski, *Laika,* 2008, sculpture / installation, mixed media [tinware, polyester resin, wood, fake fur, imitation leather]. Courtesy of *Kolekcja Regionalna Zachęty Sztuki Współczesnej w Szczecinie.*)

assumption that art is an important voice in animal studies discourse. At first glance, the story of Laika may appear to be a disgraceful incident from the past of the USSR. The truth, however, is grim: Animals are still being sent into space, not only by Russia but also by the United States and other countries. The article "Animals in Space," published on the NASA website in the section devoted to student education, starts with this: "Can fish swim in microgravity? Do bees make honey in space? Can ant farms exist on the Space Station? These are just a few of the questions scientists hope to answer by taking animals into space" (NASAexplores, 2004, para 1). The tone indicates that animal experiments are going to be continued in the future, and the article tries to convince the reader that these experiments are crucial to the development of science.

The Story of Laika and Other Space Animals

Contrary to popular belief (often repeated in the press), Laika was neither the first animal sent into space, nor was she the first mammal forced to make that trip. There were many predecessors and none of them made history. Many animals, among them many Soviet dogs, died in space—for instance Dezik and Lisa, Chizhik and Mishka, Mishka-2, Ryzhik-2, Rita, Bulba and Lisa-2, and Dzhoyna and Ryshaya (Turkina, 2014, pp. 232–235). However, Laika was the first one to achieve an orbital altitude and the only one whose death was not just a risk but a part of the plan.

As early as in 1948 a rhesus macaque named Albert flew inside a V-2 Blossom rocket. As Tara Gray from the NASA History Program Office writes: "Lack of fanfare and documentation made Albert an unsung hero of animal astronauts" (Gray, 1998, para. 2). A year after that, in June, Albert II flew into space. In December, it was Albert IV. In 1950, an unanesthetized mouse was sent into space and photographed in flight. None of these animals survived the impact. Each was dubbed a "space death," which may be seen with bitter irony as an honorable death. In 1951 a monkey named Yorick and 11 mice were recovered after an Aerobee missile flight; Yorick received extensive press attention as the first monkey to live through a space flight. In 1952 two Philippine monkeys, Patricia and Mike, were enclosed in Aerobee's nose section. Patricia was placed in a sitting position and Mike in a prone position to determine how rapid acceleration would affect them. Two mice, Mildred and Albert, were also present on this flight. The section containing all animals was safely recovered from the upper atmosphere; Patricia died about two years after the experiment and Mike died in 1967, both at the National Zoological Park in Washington, DC (Gray, 1998).

In the Soviet Union, researchers experimented with sending animals into space at virtually the same time. Rats, mice, and rabbits were used for initial tests, as one-way passengers. It was the Soviets who first sent a dog into the space. As Gray writes:

> Eventually they chose small dogs for this phase of testing. Dogs were chosen over monkeys because it was felt that they would be less fidgety in flight. A test with two dogs would allow for more accurate results. They chose females because of the relative ease of controlling waste. (Gray, 1998)

The latter notion is not supported by Turkina, who, in her research, encountered documentation suggesting that many male dogs were involuntary astronauts in Soviet Russia as well (Turkina, 2014, pp. 232–237). As Gray writes, between 1951 and 1952, Soviet rockets of the R-1 series carried nine dogs altogether, but of these space-bound hounds, only a few have been remembered by name (Gray, 1998). Some of the latter were Dezik and Tsygan, who became animal astronauts in 1951, as well as Lisa and Ryzhik, who flew in 1954 (Dubbs, 2003). According to Turkina, the first Soviet space dogs who reached celebrity status were Belka and Strelka, mostly because they were the first to come back alive from orbital flights. These events took place three years after Laika's death in 1957; however, it was Laika who eventually became an international pop culture heroine (and, to some, also a martyr). Her image is represented in visual art, children's books, comic books, song lyrics, and music videos, as well as on postage stamps. Her name is enough to evoke her character and the whole story. The names of other animals, including other dogs sent into space, do not signify as much, regardless of whether these animals died in space, died while returning from space, or survived. It is difficult to determine the causes of Laika's fame, although her name, easy to pronounce for an English native speaker, might have helped. Furthermore, as Turkina writes, Laika "quickly became an inseparable attribute of the space theme heavily favored in Soviet propaganda.... In terms of fame frequency that her name is mentioned, a parallel can be drawn between Laika and Yuri Gagarin" (Turkina, 2014, pp. 84–86). Good photographic documentation, including portraits of the animal seated in the Sputnik, some focusing on the animal's mouth, makes us see Laika's face and allows us to look her in the eyes—this potentially contributed to her image and let people identify with her or to compare her with their own dogs. Being confronted with the photographs taken before the flight, and knowing of Laika's tragic death in agony caused by equipment failure, stimulated people's imagination and empathy, as evidenced in artistic visualizations, comments, and interpretations of her story, sometimes providing its missing elements. The fact that she was matter-of-factly "sentenced to death" and that the mission had been planned in such a way that nobody had anticipated her return was outrageous to the public. In subsequent missions, the return of animals from space was usually planned, but Bars and Lisichka were killed in 1960 when their R-7 rocket exploded as it began its flight. Pchyolka and Mushka were killed in a Korabl-Sputnik 3 rocket that was blown up for political reasons: The spacecraft reentered the atmosphere on a trajectory which might have permitted foreign powers to inspect the capsule, prompting the Soviets to detonate an explosive charge during reentry (Dubbs, 2003).

Laika in Contemporary Polish Art

The popularity and achievements of the Soviet space program within the Eastern Bloc—therefore, also in Poland—were immense. Poland, under its communist government, has undoubtedly contributed to popularization of Laika's story and image. The origins of the earliest works discussed here, including Zbigniew Rogalski's painting, derive from this period. The artist evokes Laika in one of the paintings from his series created recently, well into the present, but with a clear reference to the past. In Rogalski's series of peculiar self-portrait from the years 2002–2003, showing his reflections in a fogged mirror, almost invisible, the artist recalls—using finger-drawn inscriptions on a steamy mirror surface—various heroes from his childhood. One of them is Laika, whose name is written in Cyrillic: Лайка. Among Rogalski's idols, such as musical performers Joy Division and Björk and philosophers Kant and Nietzsche, there are Soviet astronauts. We thus find Laika next to Yuri Gagarin, Gherman Titov, and Valentina Tereshkova. Rogalski devotes a painting to each of his childhood heroes. A realistically painted inscription on the steamy mirror becomes an inscription on the painting, as the surface of the mirror is identified with a painting canvas. This inscription, consisting simply of Laika's name, is the only sharp, clear, and primary element of the painting because everything else—space, objects, a human figure—can be seen only as blurry reflections in Rogalski's steamy mirror surface.

This picture is also important with regard to the properties of painting itself because the series it is a part of raises the issue of the blurring of images, recognizing natural barriers in vision—and the artist tries to find positive value in this. This purely painterly aspect can be referred metaphorically to the history of sending animals into space without noticing their suffering or at least without considering it real and meaningful. Dreams of conquering space disrupt our viewing of animals as "living beings capable of suffering and not objects," as the 1997 Polish Animal Protection Act reminds us in its very first paragraph.

The creative process is based on the concept of the artist writing on a surface of a steamy bathroom mirror using his finger. He then photographs the inscription and moves this scene onto canvas. While writing, he reveals this tiny area of the mirror, located in a thin (fingerbreadth) letter line. He removes what blocks our vision, so he allows us to see. In Rogalski's series of paintings, Laika takes a place equal not only to humans but also to great individuals such as Kant or Nietzsche. Such equalization within the structure of the artistic series expresses equalization on a psychological and emotional level. For the artist, Laika's story has a tragic overtone and reminds us that animals are victims who bear the costs of human deeds and human ambitions concerning the conquest of Earth and space. At the

Zbigniew Rogalski recalls Laika as the heroine of his childhood fascination with Soviet astronautics. (Zbigniew Rogalski, *Untitled [Laika]*, 2003, oil on canvas. Courtesy of Raster gallery, Warsaw.)

same time, Rogalski sees Laika as one of the creatures of importance in the history of the world and in his personal point of view.

The fact that animals were the first astronauts—or cosmonauts, to use the Soviet term—was also noticed by Artur Malewski, who presents Laika in his 2008 sculpture, created for the Fifth Triennale of Young Artists in the Centre of Polish Sculpture in Orońsko. Space animals, with their technology-enhanced bodies, were the first to appear in space, a region hostile to living beings—thus Malewski sees them as the first cybernetic organisms. The artist intentionally expresses ambivalence in the work: On the one hand it can be considered a monument of triumph for humankind;

on the other it is a tribute to a dog victim, Laika, for whom Sputnik 2 became a death chamber and then a coffin (personal communication with the artist, February–March 2015).

In 2010, in Malewski's individual exhibition in Wozownia Gallery in Toruń, this work was presented in a way that brought out its impact in a particularly powerful way: in a dark room with wooden pillars that made the space resemble a forest. I was circulating among dimly lit artworks; the darkness around forced me to focus on this one object only. Malewski's *Łajka* is in the form of a Sputnik capsule, modeled on the one that became Laika's coffin. I approached the sculpture-machine and encircled it to finally take a look inside a round window. Behind the glass I found a horrifying view of a dog's mouth twisted in pain. After a second I understood what the black color meant: the dog is becoming carbonized and it is the moment of her death. Laika's demise at a very high temperature, as well as her suffering, was what Malewski tried to show. And although it was not his ambition to present the death of Laika in congruence with scientific documentation, he presented the moment of her death the way he had imagined it on the basis on descriptions from the press and Wikipedia.

In Malewski's work, Laika is petrified in pain forever—forever in the moment of dying, but still alive and suffering. Malewski's work mercilessly reminds us of the most difficult and troubling moment in the whole story, visualizing what was not immortalized in photographs. I can also add that he visually reveals what was supposed to be hidden from our sight—as the scientists, the press, and the politicians presented the dog only before the flight, safe and sound. The object (it cannot be classified as a traditionally understood sculpture) implements one of the idealistic demands that define classical sculpture as a genre of art: a frozen moment, a petrified movement. Malewski perpetuates the moment that became eternity for Laika, although in the viewer's "real time" it already belongs to the past. Laika is dead and yet she is still dying. For her, the time of painful death, with her heartbeat accelerating and the temperature inside the spacecraft rising, might have seemed like eternity because pain alters the perception of time. Malewski makes Laika's dying in a cruel way eternal and

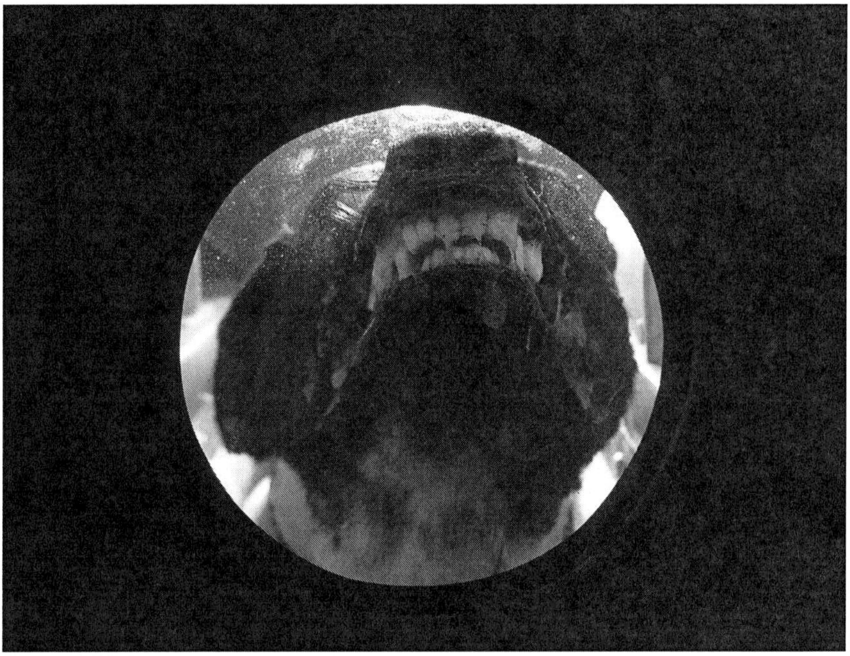

In Malewski's work, Laika is petrified in pain, forever in the moment of dying but still alive and suffering. (Artur Malewski, *Laika,* 2008, sculpture / installation, mixed media [tinware, poliester resin, wood, fake fur, imitation leather]. Courtesy of *Kolekcja Regionalna Zachęty Sztuki Współczesnej w Szczecinie.*)

he forces the viewer to observe this very moment. However, he brings up and strongly emphasizes the ethical aspect of using animals in astronautic research, appealing to viewers' empathy. This effect has been enhanced by the fact that the animal figure is placed inside the object and her agony is not visible at first sight; it becomes visible only when the viewer leans to take a look inside the Sputnik.

In Malewski's work, the immobilization in the cramped cubicle of Sputnik 2 contrasts with the spatial openness of Agata Zbylut's installation from 2011, also named after the Soviet space dog. Made in a mixed technique with the use of real canine hair, the figurine of a sitting dog was placed directly on the floor of an open exhibition hall. Laika, sitting quietly, watches a starry sky displayed on the screen placed in front of her. Laika's calmness and the mood of the scene are completely different

In Agata Zbylut's installation from 2011, Laika, sitting quietly, watches a starry sky displayed on the screen placed in front of her. (Agata Zbylut, *Laika,* 2011, object, mixed media [papier-mâché, fur, textile], DVD projection on screen. Courtesy of the National Museum in Szczecin.)

from that in Malewski's work, and Zbylut's work illustrates another moment of the story: Laika has not yet taken off, but she is already dressed in the cosmonaut attire.

This work tackles the issue of time in a totally different way: Although it is a story from the past (because Laika's story already belongs to history and to herstory), it is actually *her own* story and it evokes the future as well. The future refers not to the real time of the viewer watching the work, but to Laika's time that it presents. She is looking at the stars where her future has been written, written both in the metaphorical sense, related to faith in destiny, and in the literal sense, related to the travel that is going to transport her into the space she is looking at. Among the many dogs kept in the Moscow Institute of Aviation Medicine, Laika was the one to be chosen, although there was a better candidate, another female dog, Albina, who was more popular with the staff; when she gave birth to puppies, the researchers did not want to separate her from them (Turkina, 2014, p. 116). What is also significant for the artist is that the period of preparing for the flight might have been the happiest time in Laika's life because, in contrast to the times of her homelessness, she was fed and cared for (personal communication with the artist, February–March 2015). In Zbylut's work, stars are falling one by one from the animation of the night sky. According to popular superstition, it is a moment to make a wish. The figure of the dog staring into the sky suggests that she is making a wish. We may guess that these were daydreams about her beloved human, perhaps about Yelena Dubrovsky (a lab worker or researcher who cared for her in the laboratory; such a conjecture of Laika's love and trust is outlined in Nick Abadzis's [2007] comic book). Maybe these dreams were about a real home or about returning to the streets of Moscow where she was free. She might, however, also be daydreaming about returning to her former human guardian: Such a scenario (without any historical background and being only a conjecture or a fantasy) was depicted in Danish musician Trentemøller's music video entitled *Moan*.

All the works I have discussed so far were looked at in terms of the Soviet, and American, space programs' experiments on animals, and the place of animals as living beings in them. An analysis of this kind thus demands an inquiry about the artists' motivations to raise these ideas. Each of these works tries to commemorate in some way Laika, the female dog who died in space; all of the artists touch on the ethical aspect of the experiments on animals. Kaja Rata, in her work *Laika Come Back!* from 2014,[1] approaches the subject in a slightly different way. The artist, intrigued by the way Laika functions in pop culture (as a nice doggie who flew into space), created a funny and moving story that aims at "visualizing contrived actions regarding dispatching dogs into orbit" (personal communication with the artist, May 2015). Rata's intent was to draw viewers' attention to the issue of animal abandonment; at the same time she wanted to "do it in a light way, so no one would feel instructed and stigmatized." The universe seems to her "currently the only space where we can lose ourselves to such an extent that we lose all hope of coming back. It is as strange and unaccustomed to a human as a motorway is to a dog thrown from a car" (personal communication with the artist, May 2015). Is it even possible to talk about Laika's story without taking a stand, without condemning people or their deeds? Isn't keeping a distance still equal to taking a stand?

Rata's work takes the form of an artistic book containing a series of montages composed of photographs found on the Internet: digital collages of images of dogs, landscapes, objects, satellite photos of the Earth seen from space, technical drawings, and user manuals. The work is

Artist Kaja Rata draws viewers' attention to the issue of animal abandonment. To Rata, outer space is as strange and unaccustomed to a human as a motorway is to a dog thrown from a car. (From *Laika Come Back!*, 2014, mixed media [drawings and photomontage printed on paper]. Courtesy of the artist.)

complemented by Rata's drawings: a Sputnik redrawn from a matchbox and two portraits of Laika. The artist took the elements of collages and technical drawings from unidentified Internet sources, presenting mundane devices and activities—for example technical drawings depicting the inside of a washing machine and how to harness a dog in preparation for a space flight. In her photomontages we see portraits of various anonymous dogs dressed in an ordinary dog harness with helmet and oxygen mask, as well as images of dogs drifting in space, all reminding us of astronauts and their attributes. The way they are presented may bring an association with Trentemøller's video *Moan*, in which a dog in weightlessness is floating in a Sputnik's interior, in the body's position congruent with its eventually flying away among the stars and disappearing on the horizon, in a way becoming one of them. Rata's intention was to present dogs in her work in such a way that they would seem universal—poignant but unrecognizable as far as breed. Because of her desire to preserve this universal dog figure, the artist has not used any images of dogs familiar to her, but only those of anonymous mongrels, all found online.

In Rata's book the issue of time also plays an important role. This work connects the cult of Laika's story with contemporaneity and a vision of the future. The representation of a historical dog (Laika) is presented in the form of a drawing made by Rata, and contemporary (and future?) dogs are shown with the help of photography. Through an artfully shrewd collation of images, the artist refers to the universal figure of a dog-cyborg-astronaut whose body has become connected with the machine to fulfill humanity's dreams of conquering space, conducted under the banner of scientific research and, therefore, supposedly justifying animal experimentation in space and elsewhere. We also see a scene with dogs wandering through a black, rocky, moonlike landscape. It is perhaps a vision of the future, when dogs once sent into space settle on an as yet unknown planet, but at the same time these dogs serve as alter egos of dogs abandoned by the road or in the forest. Laika, setting off into space, has also been abandoned, sentenced to death, and therefore betrayed by her caretakers from the research station. This situation is eloquently captured by the British cartoonist Nick Abadzis in his comic *Laika,* where he presents the narration from several perspectives—for example from that of Yelena Dobrovsky, who was responsible for training the space dogs (Abadzis, 2007).

The past, the present, and the future of space conquest was, is, and is going to be the story of animal suffering in space, as well as on Earth in the laboratories during experiments. However, as Colin Burgess and Chris Dubbs (2007) note, the roles of monkeys and rats in space programs have radically shifted from that of their pioneering brethren. They are no longer animal "astronauts" pioneering in space, but rather "lab animals" seen as playing a less important role. Considering our current plans to reach Mars, though, one may wonder if animals will not be reinstated as full-fledged astronauts again—this time as the first Mars visitors and the planet's short-term inhabitants (Dubbs & Burgess, 2007, p. 374).

The works of art discussed in this chapter, all of them created during the first 15 years of the 21st century, serve as proof that Laika's history still raises moral concerns. The artists who created these works are reflecting broader social transformations through their art. More and more, artists are posing morally loaded questions about the relations between people and other animals—about animals' subjectivity and individuality, their individual and collective fate—exposing various forms of exploitation and the killing of nonhuman animals and sometimes involving themselves politically. Although animals have been present in art since prehistoric times as the first iconographic theme, since the 1960s they have more often become main characters in works of art and in artistic activities (Łagodzka, 2014). Particularly, over the past dozen or so years, art has an important place in animal studies discourse, introducing a nonverbal rhetorical means, one that behaves differently than text (whether it is scientific, journalistic, or literary). Contemporary Polish art, and more often art criticism and curatorial practices, join the discussion, which gradually changes the role and place of animals in art in a way that is significant both to art itself and to the animals as living beings. Hence dogs, as animals with a special status in many human cultures, become protagonists of not only individual works but whole exhibitions. It is highly likely that Laika's history in Polish visual art is not over yet; hopefully other animal victims of astronautic experiments will be discovered and commemorated by the artists as well. Perhaps additional pieces of art will add something of value or have yet another type of impact on viewers, interacting with resources using new means, reshaping both viewers and the art in a way of real importance to the ethical changes in human-animal relations, simultaneously enriching art itself.

Note

1. Selected images from this work can be viewed at http://cargocollective.com/kajarata/LAIKA-COME-BACK.

References

Abadzis, N. (2007). *Laika*. New York, NY: First Second.

D'Antonio, M. (2005). *A ball, a dog, and a monkey: 1957—The space race begins.* New York, NY: Simon & Schuster.

Dubbs, C. (2003). *Space dogs: Pioneers of space travel.* Lincoln, NE: iUniverse.

Dubbs, C., & Burgess, C. (2007). *Animals in space: From research rockets to the space shuttle.* New York, NY: Springer.

Dziennik Ustaw Rzeczypospolitej Polskiej [The Official Journal of Laws of the Republic of Poland]. (2015, February 26). Ustawa z dnia 15 stycznia 2015 r. o ochronie zwierząt wykorzystywanych do celów naukowych lub edukacyjnych [The law on the protection of animals used for scientific or educational purposes]. Retrieved from http://www.dziennikustaw.gov.pl/du/2015/266/1 [Accessed 28 May, 2015].

European Commission. (2015). Ban on animal testing. Retrieved from http://ec.europa.eu/growth/sectors/cosmetics/animal-testing/index_en.htm [Accessed 28 May 2015].

Gray, T. (1998). A brief history of animals in space. Retrieved from http://history.nasa.gov/animals.html [Accessed 28 May 2015].

Łagodzka, D. (2014). "Ecce Animalia": Representations of animals in art: In the net of relations and meanings. In *Ecce animalia* [Exhibition catalog]. Orońsko, Poland: Center of Polish Sculpture in Orońsko Press.

NASA. (2015). What's next for NASA? Retrieved from http://www.nasa.gov/about/whats_next.html [Accessed 28 May 2015].

NASAexplores. (2004). Animals in space. Retrieved from http://www.nasa.gov/audience/forstudents/9-12/features/F_Animals_in_Space_9-12.html [Accessed 28 May 2015].

Turkina, O. (2014). *Soviet space dogs*. London, UK: Fuel Publishing.

7

Pet Cemeteries in Poland and Beyond: Their Histories, Meanings, and Symbolism

Michał Piotr Pręgowski

Archeological records offer significant evidence of how cherished our relationship with dogs has been throughout the ages. Ceremonial burial of canines, the symbolic culmination of the interspecies bond, can be tracked back to at least 16,500 years ago (Losey et al., 2013). In the less distant, well-researched era of ancient Greece, humans openly wept for their departed dogs, buried them as family members, and expressed their affliction and bereavement in the form of epitaphs and elegies (Bodson, 2000). Similar practices were observed in the first centuries of the Middle Ages: When the beloved dog of Thierry, abbot of then French Saint-Trond from 1099 to 1107, died, the priest commemorated him in an elegy that included a very contemporary-sounding reflection: "You were laughter while you were alive, but look at the grief when you have died!" (Walker-Meikle, 2013, p. 78).

Beginning in late 13th century, however, the influence of the Catholic Church in Medieval Europe inhibited previously tolerated bereavement practices, partly due to the dogma of the immortality of the soul, which since the age of Saint Thomas Aquinas ceased to include animals. In consequence, members of other species were denied ceremonial burials, at least officially. This did not stop the folk practices of burying and even worshipping particular animals, as witnessed by the cult surrounding a Greyhound called Guinefort—and Saint Guinefort postmortem—in 13th century France (Walker-Meikle, 2013). A very similar story took place in Wales, where famed Llywelyn the Great, Prince of Gwynedd, went as far as establishing a village of Beddgelert (literally, "Gelert's Grave") to honor the beloved hound he struck down due to a horrible mistake. These examples, however, are more exceptions than the rule, as the moral climate was not conducive to organizing communal burial sites dedicated to companion animals until late 19th century.

This is not to say that every social group had to adhere to the same standards; the upper class often had their own. Widely known is the case of Boatswain, Lord Byron's Newfoundland, who was commemorated with a tombstone at the poet's ancestral home of Newstead Abbey. Not only was the dog's tombstone actually bigger than the poet's own, but Boatswain was also honored with the very famous *Epitaph to a Dog* inscribed on his grave. In Italy, a well-known naturalist, Ulisse Aldrovandi (1522–1605), reported that the Gonzaga palace, located in Mantua, alone accumulated as many as 600 canine tombstones (Grześkowiak, 2013, p. 81).

Poland was not an exception; epitaphs similar in form to that authored by Lord Byron are easily found in Polish poetry from the 16th century onward. According to Danuta Forelle and Maria Szuszkiewiczowa (1976), the inspiration for such poems was provided by the social lives of dukes, princes, and barons and their families. During the Renaissance, Baroque, and Enlightenment periods, aristocrats often kept poets as members of the court. The literary works of these poets thus reflected their benefactors' military, political, and daily lives; their family events; and, last but not least, the passing of beloved animal companions of the court. Numerous epitaphs and elegies from these periods remain, and many of them were written by renowned Polish poets of that time. Daniel Naborowski (1573–1640), a diplomat and a member of the court of magnate Janusz Radziwiłł, dedicated a long epitaph to Lewuś, the lap dog of Duchess Zofia Radziwiłłowa, decorating the poem with then fashionable references to Greek mythology. Samuel Twardowski (before 1600–1661), who gained popularity in the 17th century Polish-Lithuanian Commonwealth and who was dubbed "the Polish Virgil" by his contemporaries, wrote a touching poem about Garsonek, the dog of a certain Jakub Wojewódzki. The latter fell in the battle of Smoleńsk in 1634, and his death allegedly prompted Garsonek to die out of sorrow, an event that inspired Twardowski. Other renowned poets who wrote canine epitaphs included Jan Andrzej Morsztyn (1621–1693), a leading poet of the Polish Baroque and the author of *Nadgrobek Perlisi* (Perlisia's epitaph), as well as Franciszek Dionizy Kniaźnin (1750–1807), considered to be one of the most distinguished poets of Polish sentimentalism in the Enlightenment period, who authored *Do Jaworu. Nadgrobek suczynce Lubci* (To Jawor: The epitaph for the dam named Lubcia). The dog belonged to Duchess Izabela (1746–1835) of the influential and powerful Czartoryski family (Grześkowiak, 2013).

What is the common denominator for the Polish aristocrats and mighty Gonzaga family, as well as Lord Byron and Llywelyn the Great? Their social privilege and the capability to benefit from it. It goes without saying that for the vast majority in Western societies, the ability to publicly commemorate animal companions remained complicated until very recently.

The Emergence of the Contemporary Pet Cemetery

The winds of change began to blow in the second half of the 19th century, and the main driving forces were the secularization and urbanization of Western societies. The rise of modern capitalism brought in the new bourgeoisie, and by the end of the 19th century purebred dogs and cats, a reflection of the social status and aspirations of the middle class (McHugh, 2004), became a fixture in the cities. Being able to provide companion animals with a dignified farewell upon their death not only ceased to be a cultural taboo, but it also became a logical necessity due to spatial restrictions connected with living in a big city. It should come as no surprise that pet cemeteries are, for the most part, located near urban agglomerations; this reflects not only the sanitary need, but also a practical one, as city dwellers' possibilities with regard to companion animal burial are limited (compared to owning a piece of land or at least a suburban backyard).

Unsurprisingly, the first modern pet cemeteries were established around the bustling capital cities of the key Western, capitalist nations. London's famous Hyde Park served as an unofficial burial ground for companion animals from 1881 until 1903, and to this day it remains the resting place of roughly 300 departed animals, predominantly canines. It all began when a park gatekeeper facilitated the burial of a local family's dog, then word spread (Wolff, 2010). A small piece of land hidden in Hyde Park's total of 350 acres became the permanent resting place for a few police dogs as well, serving as proof that local authorities turned a blind eye to the existence of the unofficial pet cemetery. Protecting it from shutting down despite legal limitations is perhaps the best indication of a true cultural change taking place in Great Britain at the turn of the 20th century.

Due to the lack of clarity regarding Hyde Park's burial grounds status, Hartsdale Pet Cemetery, established in suburban New York in 1896, is considered the first official modern pet cemetery in the world. In 1899, *Cimetière des Chiens et Autres Animaux Domestiques* (Cemetery for Dogs and Other Domestic Animals) was opened in the Parisian suburb of Asnières-sur-Seine. Today there are more than 600 pet cemeteries in the United States alone (Brandes, 2009; Pierce, 2012), and cemeteries have thrived in many Western societies (Franklin, 1999, p. 93). It is worth noting that Hartsdale's original name, Hartsdale Canine Cemetery, placed the human-canine relationship above other human relationships with companion animals, as did the cemetery in Asnières-sur-Seine.

Early modern gravestones and tombs of dogs and other creatures were often ostentatious in form (Brandes, 2009; Gaillemin, 2009). This incidentally added to their historical value: Hartsdale was honored with an entry in the U.S. National Register of Historic Places as a site of profound cultural significance (and is the only pet cemetery so recognized), and *Cimetière des Chiens et Autres Animaux Domestiques* is a nationally recognized monument in France. According to Stanley Brandes, Hartsdale and other early cemeteries were at first meant to facilitate the needs of the city-dwelling upper class, as well as artists and celebrities (Brandes, 2009, p. 100). Throughout the 20th century, however, pet cemeteries became significantly democratic, open and available to everyone, regardless of their social and economic status. Here the findings of Brandes and Adrian

Franklin (1999) among others are mirrored by my field studies on American pet cemeteries in 2013–2015; premises such as Sheabel Pet Cemetery near Richmond, Kentucky, Ohio Valley Pet Cemetery in Sellersburg, Indiana, and Arley Burt Pet Cemetery in Helena, Montana, began serving local dwellers in 1960s and 1970s. Contemporary gravestones are visibly more modest than the very early and historical ones erected at Hartsdale and Asnières-sur-Seine—a testament to the down-to-earth, inclusive approach typical of recent decades and of small, local pet cemeteries.

Despite the fact that Poland has a well-documented history of paying respect to beloved animals (of the upper class), the pet cemetery concept remained virtually unknown in Poland until the fall of communism. It is worth noting, however, that the first cemetery, *Psi los* (A Dog's Life), was established in Konik Nowy near the capital city of Warsaw as early as 1991, merely two years after the restoration of democracy. Its beginnings thus mirror the growing popularity of pet cemeteries in the 1970s and 1980s West, as well as Japan (see also Ambros, 2012). Communist censorship and a limited access to cultural products and artifacts of the West are most likely to blame for the Polish delay, as suggested indirectly to the author by Witold Wojda, the proprietor and founder of *Psi los;* Wojda only found out about pet cemeteries through the free press after the disintegration of the Eastern Bloc and quickly decided Poland needed such establishments as well (Pręgowski, in press).

As Wojda writes on the *Psi los* website (www.psi-los.com), the cemetery was created for those who want to bid farewell to their animal friends in a dignified way. Cemetery services include burying companion animals and their transportation from anywhere in Poland. The latter may sound like simply a business offer, but in reality it is more of a courtesy offered by a small, family-run company, as well as a reflection of the fact that the number of pet cemeteries in Poland is still insignificant and therefore animals from all over the country are being interred at *Psi los*. As of 2015, the nation of 38.5 million people had 12 official pet cemeteries at their disposal, merely 1 per 3.2 million citizens, whereas in the United States there is roughly 1 per 0.5 million citizens.[1] Economically, this suggests both a considerable potential for the Polish market and a yet unsatisfied demand of Polish society. Willingness to bid farewell to a beloved animal in a dignified, ceremonial way seems only logical considering the depth of the relationships between Poles and their dogs, cats, and other creatures. Furthermore, many people who lose beloved animals experience a period of mourning that mirrors one experienced after the loss of a close person (Gerwolls & Labott, 1994).

Just like in the United States, France, or Great Britain, the majority of Polish cemeteries are located near big cities, supporting the hypothesis that such premises are mostly an urban phenomenon. In the countryside other burial options are readily available; in many countries (including Poland) a fairly common practice is to bury a favorite animal on one's own land, not far from the house. When organized burial is not planned, deceased animals are often left in veterinary clinics, where they are transported to rendering plants and incinerated collectively with other animal remains. At the same time, the logic of consumer-oriented, globalized, Internet-powered capitalism enables other forms of bidding farewell to be available to Poles, including a somewhat extravagant option of turning a deceased animal's ashes into diamonds; the topic of less conventional "last goodbyes" is very well covered by Jessica Pierce (2012), who writes about it in the American context.

Legal and Social Circumstances

Polish pet cemeteries are overseen by the General Veterinary Inspectorate of Poland. Until 2015 only 11 were officially registered: in Szymanów, Bydgoszcz, Sicienko, Toruń, Gorzów Wielkopolski, Ropczyce, Rzędziany, Rybnik, and Bytom, as well as the aforementioned Konik Nowy near Warsaw. Most of these cemeteries were established in the first decade of the 21st century. In January 2015 the 12th cemetery, located in Węgliska near Rzeszów in Southeastern Poland, was also included in the official records (Okrzeszowski, 2015). *Cmentarz dla zwierząt w Rzeszowie* (Animal Cemetery in Rzeszów) is run by the Social Cooperative Galicia, and its development was co-financed by the European Union under the European Social Fund.

Even though *Psi los* has been established predominantly due to Witold Wojda's feeling of obligation and duty to fellow animal lovers (Pręgowski, in press), it is not an easy task to establish a pet cemetery. In light of Polish sanitary regulations, the cemetery for animals is seen as a special kind of landfill and requires numerous permits. The legality of its operation is contingent on legally ensuring the authorities that the burial of dead animals in a particular area will not endanger human or animal health. The owners are also responsible for securing the premises from easy access by third parties, including wild and domestic animals, as well as for protecting the groundwater against pollution and/or the excessive bacterial flora that causes the decomposition process—regardless of actual proximity to any human premises. In accordance with Polish law, the direct authority responsible for the supervision of each pet cemetery is the District Veterinary Officer, or *Główny Inspektorat Weterynarii* (Główny Inspektorat Weterynarii, 2012).

It is worth noting that only some of the 12 entities registered as pet cemeteries are in fact dignified establishments dedicated directly to commemorating companion animals. The registry of the General Veterinary Inspectorate of Poland includes *Międzygminny Kompleks Unieszkodliwiania Odpadów "Pro Natura"* (Intercommunal Waste Disposal Complex "Pro Natura") in Bydgoszcz as well as *Zakład Utylizacji Odpadów* (Waste Utilization Plant) in Gorzów Wielkopolski, places of little enticement to the bereaved and mourning.

Furthermore, the obligations imposed by the law are mum on ethics and good practices; in consequence, not all cemeteries adhere to the same, high standards. This problem eventually led to establishing the *Stowarzyszenie Właścicieli Cmentarzy i Krematoriów Zwierząt w Polsce* (Association of Owners of Pet Cemeteries and Animal Crematoriums in Poland), members of which promote their take on said standards on the association's website:[2]

> The main objective of the association is to develop standards of dignified burial and cremation of our domestic animals. The main task of every cemetery should be, first and foremost, to provide the assistance and support to animal owners in difficult times. It is also

> important [to make sure] that they are not subject to persuasion or asked to make decisions under pressure—[there is] no need to force them to make decisions with long-term consequences while they are under stress. The burial (or cremation) agreements should be clear and beneficial for both [animal] and cemetery owners. Duties and obligations of both sides should be clearly stated and priced realistically ... so that the owners are not surprised, after a year or two, with excessive, additional charges after the burial. But at the same time they [animal owners] should realize that burying their favorite animal at the cemetery is associated with accepting certain obligations relating to the nature of the place, its objectives or even [our] requirement to pay land tax for where the cemetery is located. This would avoid potential, unnecessary misunderstandings. (Stowarzyszenie Właścicieli Cmentarzy i Krematoriów Zwierząt w Polsce, 2014, para. 4)

Members of the association also declare their willingness to share their know-how with everyone interested in starting a pet cemetery in Poland:

> Quite often we receive phone calls from people interested in running a pet cemetery. We surely miss cemeteries in Poznań, Kraków, Szczecin, Gdańsk, Łódź and in many other towns. We try to help everyone who contacts us: we pass on tips and tricks and, at a later stage, we can also share the complete documentation, [know-how of] necessary procedures, contacts and technologies. (Stowarzyszenie Właścicieli Cmentarzy i Krematoriów Zwierząt w Polsce, 2014, para. 3)

Such a prosocial approach should not come as a surprise; many pet cemeteries, in Poland and abroad alike, are "businesses from the heart." Furthermore, as mentioned previously, Witold Wojda's key driving force behind the establishment of *Psi los* was a sense of duty, as well as compassion. It is indeed somewhat glaring that some of the biggest Polish cities, such as Cracow, Gdańsk, Szczecin, and Poznań, do not yet have a nearby pet cemetery. However, the first harbingers of change are already visible.

Not only was a new cemetery just opened near Rzeszów, but others seem to be on the way. In 2014 local authorities of Szczecin signed an agreement to open a pet cemetery within three years (Moje Miasto Szczecin, 2014). Also in 2014, *Gazeta Pomorska* reported that the local authorities of Grudziądz are strongly considering establishing one (*Gazeta Pomorska*, 2014). Ongoing talks are taking place in Elbląg (Jatczyńska, 2014), as well as in Olsztyn, where a volunteer in a local animal shelter has tried to gather the required information and expertise (*Gazeta Olsztyńska*, 2015). Cracow, in turn, acknowledged the need for a pet cemetery as early as 2000, but political and faith-related turmoil halted the decision making until very recently; as the daily newspaper *Gazeta Krakowska* reported in May 2015, the city council unanimously approved a resolution on the creation of a local cemetery for animals, although it remains unclear exactly when it will open (Serafin, 2015).

As Brandes aptly notes, burying animals in a public cemetery is a gesture that demonstrates extraordinary devotion to these animals and attributes a degree of sacredness to them (Brandes, 2009, p. 101). Even though so far pet cemeteries are a resting place for only a fraction of Polish companion animals, the rising awareness about them cannot go unnoticed. It should not be surprising that the article from *Gazeta Krakowska,* clearly supporting the pet cemetery cause, reminds its readers that

> legally one can dispose of the animal's body with medical waste. Not many owners choose such a fate for their dog or cat. Under cover of the night they bury their animals in the backyards, near the summer houses, in Zakrzówek [lake park], in Jordan park and even in the Wolski Forest. This is, however, against the law. (Serafin, 2015)

Indeed, under the Act on Maintaining Cleanliness and Order in Municipalities (last updated in 2011), burying animals on both public and private property is against the law, the latter being punishable by a fine of up to 5000 Polish Zloty (an equivalent of roughly 1200 USD), and the former considered a criminal offense of a lesser kind. At the same time it is difficult to assess whether burying animals in public places and on one's own grounds is in fact as common as *Gazeta Krakowska* asserts; no research has been conducted so far to estimate the popularity of these practices in Poland. Furthermore, my personal observation suggests that some Poles may in fact not realize what happens to the bodies of their beloved animals; most four-legged friends either die in the veterinarian's office or are taken there by the veterinarian after euthanizing the animal at the guardian's home. The body is therefore left in the custody of someone trusted and chosen for his or her professionalism, someone intimately connected to both the grieving human and the deceased animal. One may hypothesize that this can lead to expecting or even assuming that everything "will be taken care of" with care and dignity—a presumed, and not illogical, continuation of the positive experiences with the veterinarian encountered by the individual to this point.[3]

Of course others may simply not care about the body of their dead animal at all. In fact, Internet comments with regard to pet cemeteries seem to indicate that for some, a dog is still "only a dog," while others may want to ignore the truth, half-expecting the harsh reality of the disposal process but unwilling to investigate the topic any further. Such blissful ignorance is bound to be confronted more often these days, though, as press articles about pet cemeteries now typically mention the unpleasant procedure while pointing to its alternative.

Polish and American Pet Cemeteries: Their Similarities and Differences

Changing attitudes toward companion animals in contemporary societies can be observed in numerous ways and using many research tools, although few repositories of information about such changes are as stable as pet cemeteries. Gravestone inscriptions serve as a reliable, almost permanent written record, one that can be revisited after a few years or decades. In the case of cemeteries as old as Hartsdale (est. 1896), socially significant changes are particularly easy to trace and can be analyzed gradually on numerous levels. In Poland, where the first pet cemetery was established roughly 25 years ago, such changes will be better observed with time, but even now numerous interesting observations can be made.

Canine graves are decorated with flowers and votive candles just like human graves, although Polish pet cemeteries are also home to artifacts such as toys, collars, and favorite snacks. (Photo by Michał Piotr Pręgowski.)

For the most part, pet cemeteries can be looked at from two main perspectives: interspecific and cross-cultural. The interspecific perspective would then look at similarities and differences between pet cemeteries and human cemeteries, whereas the cross-cultural perspective would observe the customs and symbolism of pet cemeteries in different countries, such as, for example, Poland and the United States.[4] This chapter includes both perspectives.

Although the modern pet cemetery is known in many cultures and started almost simultaneously in Great Britain, the United States, and France, it can be argued that Poles see it as a predominantly American concept and are thus chiefly influenced by the American understanding of pet cemeteries. This can be witnessed, for example, by the choice of photographs accompanying press articles about pet cemeteries, by the interest of the Association of Owners of Pet Cemeteries and Animal Crematoriums in Poland in the (very American) recognition of military and police dogs, and also by cemetery owners' personal inspirations. Arkadiusz Żmuda from Social Cooperative Galicia, responsible for the 2015 opening of the pet cemetery in Rzeszów, admits such openly and declares the intention to design and maintain the premises of the cemetery in the "American style" (Okrzeszowski, 2015). Looking for similarities and differences between a relatively new (25-year-old) concept in a post-communist country and one with almost 120 years of history in a country with an even older democracy thus seems plausible and interesting.

In their general appearance, pet cemeteries—old and new, Polish and American—are rather close to human cemeteries, although the graves and gravestones are understandably smaller (Brandes, 2009; Pręgowski, in press). Pet cemeteries often seem less somber than their human counterparts, predominantly due to their location, which is often in a spacious field or on the edge of a forest, far from the city and its noise and ubiquitous rush. This applies to both Poland and the United States; for example, Sheabel Pet Cemetery in rural Kentucky is located in a forest clearing, just like *Psi los* in Konik Nowy near Warsaw and the newly established cemetery in Rakszawa near Rzeszów. *Granica* (The Border), located on a hill in Ropczyce, offers

Pet Memorial Day, an informal day of remembrance of departed companion animals. Many people in Poland lay flowers and toys and light candles on the graves of deceased animals, just as they do on All Saints' Day for their human family members. (Photo by Michał Piotr Pręgowski.)

a beautiful view of the neighboring valley, whereas *Łąka Pupila* near Piła reflects its location in its name, translatable as Pet's Meadow.

Companion animal graves and tombstones are often constructed from the same materials as the human ones. Marble, granite, and other stones, typically used for the graves of deceased humans, are often the go-to material at pet cemeteries as well. Furthermore, both types of gravestones carry basic information about the ones who passed away: their name and age (dates of birth and death), as well as some details about the relationship with the bereaved ones. In both types of places the graves are decorated with flowers and votive candles, although pet cemeteries are also home to other artifacts, such as toys, collars, and favorite snacks (Pręgowski, 2014, in press). In Poland many animal graves are visited throughout the year just like the human ones, as proven by the appearance of fresh toys, candles, and flowers on the graves, and the general tidiness of the latter. The living commemorate the dead on their birthdays and death anniversaries, as well as on holidays such as Christmas.

A particular pet cemetery–related custom has emerged in Poland. All Saints' Day, a solemn holiday celebrated on November 1 by the Roman Catholic Church and various Protestant denominations, bears particular significance for Poles. On that day, close and distant relatives of deceased humans gather at their graves to pay respects, lay flowers, and light a votive candle in their memory. Unlike in the United States, All Saints' Day is an official public holiday in Poland. It is therefore interesting—and telling, from a sociological point of view—that such an important social ritual is mirrored by Pet Memorial Day, an informal but well-known day of remembrance among animal lovers. It is held in Poland on the first Sunday of October after October 4. This date is meaningful for two reasons: it is the Feast Day of Saint Francis of Assisi, the patron saint of animals, and it is World Animal Day, the international day of action for animal rights and welfare.

There are also similarities between pet cemeteries and human cemeteries in the United States that are not found in Poland. One of them concerns the use of religious symbols such as the Christian Cross and the Star of David. According to Brandes (2009), the inclusion of religious sentiments and sectarian symbols started after World War II and includes explicit mentioning of heaven, as well as sacred entities such as God and Jesus Christ, and sometimes even quotes from the Bible. One of Hartsdale's gravestones bears a Celtic cross and the inscription, "We will see you in Heaven!," whereas another entrusts dogs to God's care and yet another states that the animal "went to heaven on Yom Kippur Day" (Brandes, 2009, pp. 108–109). My field research on rural pet cemeteries in the United States confirms this trend: Frissie (1984–2000), interred at the Ohio Valley Pet Cemetery, is a "Little Angel in Heaven," and the farewell to Little Thunder (1995–2005) urges, "See you in Heaven." A message to Sam at the same cemetery says, "See you in Heaven. Love, Mommy," whereas Dana's (1996–2011) people state, "After the loss of two God gave us you. So until then, Love." At Sheabel cemetery in Kentucky and Arley Burt in Montana, visual attributes of faith, such as crosses, angels, and depictions of Christ, are popular choices. In comparison, uses of the Christian Cross and references to biblical content are very scarce at Polish pet cemeteries while overwhelmingly popular at those for humans.

What to make of this noticeable absence and of limiting religious references to an occasional mention of heaven? It seems likely that these omissions are intentional, as if Poles were afraid to offend their brothers and sisters in faith; it should be noted that the Polish Catholic Church is at best divided when it comes to contemporary human-animal relationships and some priests, such as, for example, Salesian brother Damian Wojciechowski (2013), superficially blame dogs and cats for low childbirth rates in the country. The motivation to lead a cautious coexistence with those not ready to accept the pet cemetery concept is present in the views and comments of some pet cemetery owners, including Witold Wojda of *Psi los* (personal communication, July 2014) and Tomasz Jagielski of Wrocław's *Tęczowy Most*. Asked about the topic by a journalist, Jagielski put it bluntly, stating that he does not want to offend anyone nor to force anything on anyone, so therefore the form of the gravestone should be neutral (Dzikowska, 2015). It also goes without saying that so far no official religious mortuary rites are available for companion animals in Poland.

This is not to say that Polish canine guardians do not believe in the animal afterlife. But because stating, "Our baby girl sleeps in Jesus"—as

Inclusion of religious sentiments and sectarian symbols is very common in U.S. pet cemeteries but very rare in their Polish counterparts—a glaring cultural difference. (Photo by Michał Piotr Pręgowski.)

did the Tungett family for their companion named Sam (1973–1983, buried in Sellersburg, Indiana)—would not be a widely accepted choice in predominantly Catholic Poland, animal lovers express their beliefs about animal afterlife less directly. This need for indirection leads us to the ubiquitousness of the rainbow-colored pinwheels, a true staple in Polish pet cemeteries (and an item readily used in American ones). For many it symbolizes the popular Rainbow Bridge, a passage to a green meadow reminiscent of Eden for companion animals, where all departed dogs, cats, and similar creatures go to frolic and wait before their humans finally join them. The rainbow pinwheel can therefore be considered a symbol of hope and inclusive transcendence, as well as a means of circumventing a taboo (Pręgowski, 2014, in press).

The belief in animal immortality or some other form of continuation of existence is also present in gravestone inscriptions. Sabinka (1995–2007), buried at *Psi los,* is commemorated by a dedication from her bereaved people: "You were our joyful spark and a friend. You left [us with] void and pain, but you will remain in our hearts forever. Wait for us. Till later." At the same cemetery Dinka (1998–2013) is asked via her gravestone inscription to wait for her people "by the Rainbow Bridge." The guardian of Dina, a rescue who lived from 1994 to 2006, honors her with an aphorism: "When our Best Friend departs we are left with Hope that inside the Rainbow Bridge gates he is as happy as always."[5]

Exceptions to any rule usually emerge over time, and such is the case with Polish pet gravestones. The gravestone of Ares at *Granica* cemetery in Ropczyce not only reveals that Ares lived for 13 years but also quotes Ecclesiastes 3:19 and reminds us that "all have the same breath."

Nevertheless, a glaring difference does exist in the ways in which Poles and Americans define the human-animal relationship itself. Early monument inscriptions in American pet cemeteries generally conveyed bare facts and rarely expressed emotions, and they typically referred to dead dogs as "friends" who were "beloved"; kinship and family terms started to appear on dog gravestones after World War II (Brandes, 2009, p. 106). According to Brandes, the phenomenon of denoting family or kinship ties, including calling dogs "babies," "kids," "girls," "boys," "sons," and "daughters" and their guardians "mommies" and "daddies" (rather than "owners" or "masters"), intensified in the United States in the 1990s. This time period mirrors the emergence of the pet cemetery in Poland per se, yet so far only a small number of gravestone inscriptions describe the human-canine relationship in terms of kinship or surrogate parenthood. In Poland, companion animals are predominantly described as "friends," albeit usually "best friends" or "faithful friends"; words such as "mom," "dad," "parent," and, even less likely, "son" or "daughter," hardly ever occur in these inscriptions (Pręgowski, in press). Another rare linguistic practice is providing the animal with the family surname, therefore acknowledging the kinship in a simple yet very powerful way; whereas in Polish pet cemeteries seeing Pimpuś Branicki is a rarity, American pet cemeteries abound with beloved companions' names presented with the human family's surname. Buzzy Worrell, Brandy Key, Rocky Reynold, Susie Moore, Brandi and Cassie Dunn (at Sheabel near Richmond, Kentucky); Sunny Snyder, Keesha Spruch, and Mitzy Sparkman (at Ohio Valley Pet Cemetery in Sellersburg, Indiana); and Tipy Davis and Pooh Pui Finstad (at Arley Burt Pet Haven in Helena, Montana) are just a few examples of this practice.

Does this mean that Poles do not consider dogs to be members of the family? Do they not maintain the physical and emotional closeness that characterizes kinship? Social practices, including some presented earlier in this book, suggest that they do. At times this can even be observed at the cemeteries, where some canine gravestones include "family" as a self-definition of the grieving Polish guardians, whereas the grieved one is described merely as a "friend"—a clear indication of struggling with terms, but not feelings. Such stumbling should be considered predominantly cultural (i.e., the result of prevailing religious beliefs and difficulty assessing what is socially acceptable) and lingual. It should be noted that the cliché of the dog being "man's best friend" is rooted in Polish perhaps even more deeply than it is in English, so it should come as no surprise that many bereaved guardians readily use it on gravestones. At the same time it will be very interesting to observe how fast the winds of change will blow; it is noteworthy that Maxio Litwiński (1999–2012), Fruzia Kazimierska (1996–2010), Nirvana Kielar (2001–2014), Surya Kielar (2005–2015), and the aforementioned Pimpuś Branicki (1996–2011) were interred in recent years. This, in connection with a clearly rising demand for pet cemeteries, amounts to a fascinating phenomenon to observe in the coming years.

Most social customs connected with Polish and American pet cemeteries are (unsurprisingly) similar to those previously reserved for humans. Pet cemeteries and human cemeteries share a lot of symbolism and use some of the same artifacts. Furthermore, many social practices characteristic of Polish pet cemeteries are the same as or very similar to those known and performed in the United States. However, it is safe to assume that one particular practice is unlikely to be implemented in Poland anytime soon: A small but growing social movement in the West, particularly in the United States, is lobbying for "whole family cemeteries" that would allow pets and humans to be buried together, in the same grave.

This would be a very difficult pill to swallow for many religious countries around the world, including Poland, where the Roman Catholic Church remains a formidable intellectual and political influence and prohibits the burial of animals alongside humans. As mentioned at the beginning of the chapter, since the time of Saint Thomas Aquinas, the official Catholic interpretation of the Bible claims that only humans possess

Whereas U.S. pet cemeteries abound with canine names presented with the human family's surname, graves such as that of Maxio Litwiński are still a rarity in Poland. (Photo by Michał Piotr Pręgowski.)

immortal souls and only humans can be buried in holy ground. Perhaps this interpretation will change some day; at the dawn of the human-canine relationship, ceremonial co-burial was not abnormal, as witnessed for example at Paleolithic sites in Belgium, the Ukraine, and Russia (Germonpré et al., 2009). Furthermore, the Bible is not unequivocal when it comes to other beings, as the gravestone of Ares at Ropczyce and its reference to Ecclesiastes 3:19 remind us. In the New International Translation of the Bible, this fragment reads as follows:

> For what happens to people also happens to animals—a single event happens to them: just as someone dies, so does the other. In fact, they all breathe the same way, so that a human being has no superiority over an animal. All of this is pointless.

Regardless of cultural differences and similarities between the pet cemetery practices in post-communist Poland and the contemporary United States, the Ecclesiastes quote surely plucks at the heartstrings of many canine enthusiasts in both countries, particularly those who consider companion animals their best friends and family.

Notes

1. This estimate is based on the population of the United States (318.9 million in 2014) and the "more than 600 pet cemeteries" reported by Brandes (2009) and Pierce (2012). Although employing the ratio of pet cemeteries per capita may seem a bit awkward, it is a much better means of comparison than the ratio of pet cemeteries per an estimated and likely very inaccurate number of companion animals in a given country.
2. More information, in Polish, is available at www.cmentarz-zwierzat.pl/?page=G1_stowarzyszenie [Accessed 20 January 2016].
3. This is reflected by the story behind the establishment of *Granica* (The Border), the pet cemetery in Ropczyce. The premises are run by a local veterinarian whose inspiration came directly from his clients. As the cemetery website reports, many of them asked about "doing something" with the departed animal, expecting a dignified treatment of the body (Granica, 2009).
4. This chapter stems from an ongoing research project started in 2012. The project consists of fieldwork in Poland and abroad. To date, particular emphasis has been placed on the *Psi los* cemetery because it is the oldest pet cemetery in Poland and on rural American pet cemeteries because they serve small communities rather than large cities. Three research field trips in Poland (2012–2014) have been discussed in detail in two separate articles: one in the book *Pies też człowiek? Relacje psów i ludzi we współczesnej Polsce* (A dog's life? On humans and canines in contemporary Poland; published by WN Katedra in 2014) and another in an upcoming collection edited by Margo DeMello and titled *Mourning Animals.* A few observations presented in this chapter derive from my past research and are duly referenced, while others come from ongoing U.S. pet cemetery studies, started in 2013, as well as from my resumed research in Poland.
5. This example also shows that the Rainbow Bridge can symbolize both the passage and the land where all beloved companion animals go. The use of capital letters in the quote mirrors their use in Polish.

References

Ambros, B. R. (2012). *Bones of contention: Animals and religion in modern Japan*. Honolulu: University of Hawai'i Press.

Bodson, L. (2000). Motivations for pet-keeping in Ancient Greece and Rome: A preliminary survey. In A. Podberscek, E. Paul, & J. Serpell (Eds.), *Companion animals and us: Exploring the relationships between people and pets* (pp. 27–41). Cambridge, UK: Cambridge University Press.

Brandes, S. (2009). The meaning of American pet cemetery gravestones. *Ethnology, 48*(2), 99–118.

Dzikowska, J. (2015, January 27). *Na zwierzęcym cmentarzu. Pogrzeby z muzyką, przemowami, trumnami ze szkła* [On an animal cemetery: Burials with music, speeches and coffins made of glass]. Retrieved from http://m.wroclaw.gazeta.pl/wroclaw/1,106542,17307767,Na_zwierzecym_cmentarzu__Pogrzeby_z_muzyka__przemowami_.html [Accessed 23 May 2015].

Forelle, D., & Szuszkiewiczowa, M. (1976). *Psie nagrobki pięknie rymowane. Psia księga*. [Canine gravestones well rhymed: A dog book]. Warsaw, Poland: Nasza Księgarnia.

Franklin, A. (1999). *Animals and modern cultures: A sociology of human-animal relations in modernity*. London, UK: Sage.

Gaillemin, B. (2009). Vivre et construire la mort des animaux: Le cimetière d'Asnières [Living and constructing the death of animals: The cemetery of Asnières]. *Ethnologie Française, 39*(3)/2009, 495–507. http://dx.doi.org/10.3917/ethn.093.0495

Gazeta Olsztyńska. (2015, February 21). *Cmentarz dla zwierząt mógłby powstać pod Dobrym Miastem* [A pet cemetery could be established in Dobre Miasto]. Retrieved from http://olsztyn.wm.pl/248707,Cmentarz-dla-zwierzat-moglby-powstac-pod-Dobrym-Miastem.html#axzz3bOpcw971 [Accessed 23 May 2015].

Gazeta Pomorska. (2014, November 2). *Cmentarz dla zwierząt w Grudziądzu? Jest taki pomysł* [A pet cemetery in Grudziądz? There is such an idea]. Retrieved from http://www.pomorska.pl/apps/pbcs.dll/article?AID=/20141102/GRUDZIADZ01/141039819 [Accessed 23 May 2015].

Germonpré, M., Sablin, M. V., Stevens, R. E., Hedges, R. E. M., Hofreiter, M., Stiller, M., & Després, V. R. (2009). Fossil dogs and wolves from Palaeolithic sites in Belgium, the Ukraine and Russia: Osteometry, ancient DNA and stable isotopes, *Journal of Archaeological Science, 36*(2), 473–490. http://dx.doi.org/10.1016/j.jas.2008.09.033

Gerwolls, M. K., & Labott, S. M. (1994). Adjustment to the death of a companion animal, *Anthrozoös, 7*(3), 172–187. http://dx.doi.org/10.2752/089279394787001826

Główny Inspektorat Weterynarii. (2012). *Cmentarze dla zwierząt towarzyszących znajdujące się pod nadzorem Inspekcji Weterynaryjnej* [Companion animal cemeteries under the supervision of the veterinary inspectorate]. Retrieved from http://www.wetgiw.gov.pl/index.php?action=art&a_id=4063 [Accessed 23 May 2015].

Granica. (2009). *O nas* [About us]. Retrieved from http://www.cmentarz-dla-zwierzat.pl/ [Accessed 20 January 2016].

Grześkowiak, R. (2013). *Amor curiosus. Studia o osobliwych tematach dawnej poezji erotycznej* [Amor curiosus: Studies on peculiar topics in ancient erotic poetry]. Warsaw, Poland: Muzeum Pałac w Wilanowie.

Jatczyńska, N. (2014, March 11). *Chcą, by w mieście powstał cmentarz dla zwierząt* [They want a pet cemetery in town]. Retrieved from http://dziennikelblaski.pl/193678,Chca-by-w-miescie-powstal-cmentarz-dla-zwierzat.html#axzz3bPbsHTHR [Accessed 23 May 2015].

Losey, R. J., Garvie-Lok, S., Leonard, J. A., Katzenberg, M. A., Germonpré, M., Nomokonova, T., … Savel'ev, N. A. (2013). Burying dogs in ancient Cis-Baikal, Siberia: Temporal trends and relationships with human diet and subsistence practices. *PLoS ONE, 8*(5), e63740. http://dx.doi.org/10.1371/journal.pone.0063740

McHugh, S. (2004). *Dog.* London, UK: Reaktion Books.

Moje Miasto Szczecin. (2014, August 19). *Cmentarz dla zwierząt w Szczecinie powstanie w ciągu trzech lat. Umowa podpisana* [Pet cemetery in Szczecin will be established within three years: The agreement is signed]. Retrieved from http://www.mmszczecin.pl/artykul/cmentarz-dla-zwierzat-w-szczecinie-powstanie-w-ciagu-trzech,2702838,art,t,id,tm.html [Accessed 23 May 2015].

Okrzeszowski, M. (2015, January 16–18). Godne pożegnanie ze zwierzakiem [A dignified farewell]. *Nowiny,* pp. 10–11.

Pierce, J. (2012). *The last walk: Reflections on our pets at the end of their lives.* Chicago, IL: University of Chicago Press.

Pręgowski, M. P. (2014). Największy, najukochańszy. Ostatnie pożegnania opiekunów z psami [The greatest and most beloved: The last goodbyes of dogs' guardians with their companions]. In M. P. Pręgowski & J. Włodarczyk (Eds.), *Pies też człowiek? Relacje ludzi i psów we współczesnej Polsce* [A dog's life? On humans and canines in contemporary Poland] (pp. 301–327). Gdańsk, Poland: WN Katedra.

Pręgowski, M. P. (in press). All the world and a little bit more: Pet cemetery practices and contemporary relations between humans and their companion animals. In M. DeMello (Ed.), *Mourning animals*. East Lansing: Michigan State University Press. [Manuscript in press]

Serafin, D. (2015, May 13). *Kraków. Powstanie cmentarz dla zwierząt* [Cracow: A pet cemetery will be established]. Retrieved from http://www.gazetakrakowska.pl/artykul/3860849,krakow-powstanie-cmentarz-dla-zwierzat,id,t.html [Accessed 23 May 2015].

Stowarzyszenie Właścicieli Cmentarzy i Krematoriów Zwierząt w Polsce. (2014). Stowarzyszenie [The association]. Retrieved from http://www.cmentarz-zwierzat.pl/?page=G1_stowarzyszenie [Accessed 20 January 2016].

Walker-Meikle, K. (2013). *Medieval dogs*. London, UK: The British Library.

Wojciechowski, D. (2013). *Ratujmy pieski!* (Let's save doggies!). Retrieved from http://www.deon.pl/wiadomosci/komentarze-opinie/art,618,ratujmy-pieski.html [Accessed 23 May 2015].

Wolff, S. (2010, June 10). The pet cemetery of Hyde Park [London-In-Sight weblog]. Retrieved from http://londoninsight.wordpress.com/2010/10/06/pet-cemetery-hyde-park [Accessed 23 May 2015].

Contributors

Dorota Łagodzka is an art historian, and a researcher and lecturer at the Faculty of "Artes Liberales," University of Warsaw, where she teaches a course titled Animals in Art and Visual Culture. Łagodzka is a PhD candidate at the Institute of Art, Polish Academy of Sciences, and the recipient of two research grants awarded by the Polish National Science Centre (NCN) for projects titled "The Importance of Animal Studies for Culture Studies in Poland" (together with Anna Barcz) and "The Change of Animals' Status in Contemporary Art" (individually). Łagodzka has served as curator for numerous art exhibitions, including "Ecce Animalia" at the Museum of Contemporary Sculpture in Oronsko. She writes and serves as coeditor for *Artmix* magazine and blogs for "Nie-zła sztuka" and "Animal Studies PL."

Agnieszka Orłowska is an experienced dog trainer, certified by the Polish Kennel Club since 1992 as an assistant for evaluating working trials and conformation shows. She has been a member of the Polish Ethological Association since 2006. Orłowska founded the Alteri Assisted Therapy Association in 2002 and served as its chair from 2002 to 2005. From 2005 to 2009 she served as chair and a board member of the Alteri Foundation, which trains assistance dogs for persons with mobility impairments. The author of numerous articles in the international specialist press, Orłowska is a popular speaker at Polish and international seminars and conferences.

Michał Piotr Pręgowski is a sociologist and assistant professor at the Warsaw University of Technology. He is also a grantee in the Fulbright Scholar-in-Residence Program and was a visiting professor at Eastern

Kentucky University in its Animal Studies program from 2014 to 2015. Together with Justyna Włodarczyk, he is the coeditor of *Pies też człowiek? Relacje psów i ludzi we współczesnej Polsce* (A dog's life? On humans and canines in contemporary Poland), published in 2014. Pręgowski's upcoming book, *Companion Animals in Everyday Life: Situating Human-Animal Engagement Within Cultures,* will be published by Palgrave Macmillan later in 2016. His research interests include the social construction of dogs in the contemporary West, especially their naming and training, as well as social practices with regard to commemorating companion animals.

Małgorzata Rutkowska specializes in literary studies and is an assistant professor in the Department of English, Maria Curie Skłodowska University in Lublin. Her research interests include British and American travel writing in the 19th and 20th centuries, animal studies, and representations of the human-animal bond in literature. Rutkowska is the author of *In Search of America: The Image of the United States in Travel Writing of the 1980's and 1990's* (Maria Curie-Sklodowska University Press, 2006), a study which examines generic conventions in contemporary travel books and analyzes the way in which travel writers construct provincial America.

Justyna Włodarczyk received her PhD in American literature from the University of Warsaw (UW). She also holds a master's degree in cultural studies from the College of Interdisciplinary Studies in the Humanities at the UW. Włodarczyk currently is an assistant professor at the Institute of English Studies at the UW. She is an alumnus of the Fulbright program and worked on her doctoral dissertation as a junior Fulbright scholar at the University of Indianapolis. Włodarczyk is also a recipient of the Animals and Society Institute/Wesleyan Animal Studies fellowship in human-animal studies. Her current research project concerns the history of discourses of animal training read through a biopolitical framework.

Agnieszka Wojtków holds a master's degree in pedagogy. Her professional experience includes working in the dog-assisted therapy field from 2006 to 2013, where she was responsible for developing programs for socially challenged children. During this time she developed a program to help children with cynophobia. Wojtków began training dogs in 2011, and in 2012 she earned her behaviorist certification from the Centre of Applied Pet Ethology (COAPE). She also serves as the vice president of *Fundacja Adopcje Malamutów,* a nongovernmental organization devoted to finding homes for abandoned sled dogs in Poland.

Index